'The economic growth of China to become the second biggest economy in the world has also meant the globalization of Chinese investment. Researchers looking at work and employment have studied the influence of Chinese state and private capital in other parts of the world, but little has been written about South America. *China and Globalization in the Amazon* fills that gap admirably. Brazil as the dominant economy in the region stands out as the leading destination for Chinese investments. This book uses both qualitative and quantitative analysis, and four in-depth case studies, to examine the reality of Chinese work and employment practices in Brazil. The cases show common and divergent practices; perhaps more of the former than latter. The common themes of Chinese expats permeating the entire management and supervisory organization of these companies will be familiar to China researchers. The human resource management system is that of a Chinese enclave, which decides the local affairs on a global basis. But workers use social connections and familial bonds, to circulate around the labour market and apply pressure on this system. The high quality of interview material and analysis makes this a must read for all interested in Global China.'

Chris Smith, Emeritus Professor of Organisation Studies and Comparative Management, Royal Holloway University of London

'*China and Globalization in the Amazon* is an essential contribution to unveiling the connections between two critical regions in the world: The Amazon and China. Cleiton Maciel was one of the pioneers in the study of the Chinese presence in the Amazon. In this monograph, the reader will find a good overview of current China labour issues and how the Amazon became the destiny of many Chinese factories. But mainly, the reader will come across rigorous and sophisticated primary research. The author interviewed shop floor and administrative workers, managers, policymakers, and Chinese workers. He immersed himself in the universe of four factories, and the result is an engaging account that provides an in-depth picture of the labour cultures, conflicts, and negotiations. This book is a must-read for everyone interested in issues related to labour, Chinese migration, the Amazon and China as a whole.'

Rosana Pinheiro-Machado, Professor, School of Geography, University College Dublin, Ireland

'The rapid global expansion of Chinese capital in the last decade has started to reshape global political economy and production regimes. The book, *China and Globalization in the Amazon*, is among the small but rising literature that attempts to understand the behavior of Chinese multinational corporations and its impact on labor in the global economy. Based on multiple years of ethnographic research in four Chinese manufacturing plants in Manaus, Brazil, the book finds a Chinese model of production that differs from Western models in important aspects particularly the imports of almost all production inputs from China and resultant "matrix Taylorism" in the labor process. Coupled with this Chinese production model is the centralization of human resource functions and heavy use of expatriates for managerial and technical positions. These features of Chinese production and management, however, have resulted in deskilling, loss of voice, inferior pay, and precarity among the Brazilian workers. The rich details of this book greatly contribute to our understanding of Chinese investment in South America, and the findings are of important theoretical and practical implications. I highly recommend this book for anyone interested in Chinese investment in the global south.'

Mingwei Liu, Associate Professor and Co-Director, Center for Global Work and Employment School of Management and Labor Relations, Rutgers University, USA

'Professor Cleiton Maciel's research focuses on the dynamics of two crucial aspects of the present Global South: China's entry into Latin America and the tremendous changes it causes in ecosystems such as the Amazon. Through extensive sociological studies, Professor Cleiton Maciel reveals that the Chinese presence in the Brazilian Amazon is not homogenous but rather diversified and distinctive. Researchers, students, and practitioners who are interested in the effects of Beijing's industrialization on the rest of the globe will find this publication extremely useful. One of the most significant things to understand about worldwide changes today is the relationship between the environment and the development of new business models. This book is an excellent resource for studying these topics.'

Fernando Brancoli, Professor of International Relations, Federal University of Rio de Janeiro, Brazil

'Cleiton Maciel's book deals extensively with the Chinese presence in the Manaus Industrial Park, as part of the context of the last few decades of Chinese companies' evolving globalization. It focuses especially on ethnographic aspects of the Chinese expatriate managers and workers who, in the Amazon, helped to implement this expansion, describing in detail the cultural impacts on both Chinese and Brazilians. I believe this is the most in-depth work that addresses the presence and socioeconomic consequences of Chinese globalization wave in Brazil and, more specifically, in the Amazon region.'

Denis Benchimol Minev, Economist and Director President of Bemol

'The Chinese presence in Brazil, and in particular in the Amazon, is part of an overall strategy of investment expansion in South America involving geopolitical, economic and industrial interests whose lines are set out in the Belt and Road Initiative project. Cleiton Maciel's book makes a pioneering contribution to the understanding of the Chinese expansion process on a global scale by investigating how Chinese investments were made in the Manaus Industrial Park, in the heart of the Amazon rainforest, and how those factories were operated and managed under Chinese control. The research conducted by the author reveals, on one hand, the birth of a Chinese model of production and management based, above all, on the process of expatriation of Chinese to Manaus. On the other hand, the impacts of Chinese factories on local workers. The book highlights both the place and the role of the Amazon in the Chinese globalization process and the adoption of a production and management model that, through expatriation, seeks cost reduction and global control of the Chinese factories scattered throughout the world.'

Izabel Valle, Professor of Sociology,
Federal University of Amazonas, Brazil

'*China and Globalization in the Amazon* is must read to understand China's economic expansion policy in the world scenario, especially in Brazil and in the Amazon region. Brazil, South America's largest economy, stands out as a major pole of attraction for Chinese investments in the region (around 50%), especially in the sectors such as infrastructure, mining, energy, oil and gas, technology, and direct participation in the Manaus Industrial Park, located in the state of Amazonas, the heart of the Amazon. In this book, Cleiton Maciel, a researcher and well-versed in the reality of the Amazon, his place of origin and life experience, reveals the social impacts of this process. Using a pioneering sociological survey among national workers, expatriate Chinese, and union members, the author analyzes socioeconomic data, investigates changes in production systems, and shows the social, cultural, and economic consequences of the arrival of the Chinese, such as tight control over workers, low wages, centralized decision-making in the Chinese headquarters, and clashes with Brazilian labor laws. A remarkable, engaging book, succinctly and deeply written. Not to be missed!'

José Fernandes de Oliveira, Economist and Former IT Manager at
companies in the Manaus Free Trade Zone

'*Chinese Globalization in the Amazon* is an extraordinary work focused on analyzing the Chinese investment process at the Manaus Free Trade Zone. Using a variety of methodological approaches, the book manages to elucidate this process, its logic and dynamics, as well as its implications on Brazilian workers and their relations with labor unions. Addressing issues such as salaries and benefits, working conditions, qualification, forms of organization and work management, as well as, in a prominent form, the role played by expatriate workers, Cleiton Maciel sheds light on a reality that is still virtually unknown. By defending the emergence of "a Chinese model of production, with specific industrial and managerial characteristics" with significant changes on labor, the study reveals the enclave character of these investments; the companies have neither autonomy nor strong relations with the local economy. They rely primarily on Chinese inputs, while their strategy is based on precarious and rigidly managed labor, configuring what the author calls "matrix taylorism". Therefore, the study shows that, like other forms of international capital investment, the Chinese one is based on control and on simplified and poorly paid work, but it does so using its habits, culture, and traditional forms of conceiving the company and work. In other words, "China business" changes the form, but the content remains the same old over-exploitation of labor.'

Marcia Leite, Professor of the Friedrich Engels Chair, División de Ciencias Sociales y Humanidades, UAM Cuajimalpa, Mexico

CHINA AND GLOBALIZATION IN THE AMAZON

China and Globalization in the Amazon examines Chinese investment in the Global South, with particular attention to industrial activity in Latin America. Based on ethnographic work conducted in several Chinese factories in the Amazon region of Brazil, whether private, partially private, or state-owned, it explores the impact of these factories on the lives of workers, specifically on wages, laws, and labor benefits, as well as the relationship between management and workers. Drawing on interviews with Brazilian workers, expatriate Chinese workers, union leaders, and factory managers, the author identifies a Chinese production model and sheds light on the implementation of externally defined work regimes that showed little engagement with the workforce in the region, together with practices that resulted in a technical or bureaucratic relationship with the worker, and the emergence of lower wages than the local average, as well as few concessions on labor benefits. A study of Chinese globalization and industrial expansion in the developing world, and the reactions of workers to the Chinese model of management, this volume will be of interest to scholars of the sociology of work and organizations, globalization, development studies, and politics.

Cleiton Maciel Brito is Adjunct Professor of Sociology at the Federal University of Grande Dourados. He was born in Manacapuru, a small town in the state of Amazonas. He earned his PhD in Sociology from the Federal University of São Carlos. He received an award for his thesis from the Coordination for the Improvement of Higher Education Personnel (CAPES), an agency of the Federal Government of Brazil. He has published several articles and book chapters on globalization, the China–Brazil relationship, and Amazonian studies.

Global Connections

Series Editor

Robert Holton

Global Connections builds on the multi-dimensional and continuously expanding interest in globalization, focusing on 'connectedness' and providing accessible, concrete studies across a broad range of areas such as social and cultural life, and economic, political and technological activities. Interdisciplinary in approach, the series moves beyond abstract generalities and stereotypes: 'Global' is considered in the broadest sense of the word, embracing connections between different nations, regions and localities, including activities that are trans-national, and trans-local in scope; 'connections' refers to movements of people, ideas, resources, and all forms of communication as well as the opportunities and constraints faced in making, engaging with, and sometimes resisting globalization.

Titles in the series:

Teaching Practices in a Global Learning Environment
An Interdisciplinary Take on International Education
Hanne Tange

Public Space Democracy
Performative, Visual and Normative Dimensions of Politics in a Global Age
Edited by Nilüfer Göle

China and Globalization in the Amazon
Workers, Expatriates, and the Chinese Production Model
Cleiton Maciel Brito

For more information about this series, please visit: www.routledge.com/Global-Connections/book-series/ASHSER1306

CHINA AND GLOBALIZATION IN THE AMAZON

Workers, Expatriates, and the Chinese Production Model

Cleiton Maciel Brito

Routledge
Taylor & Francis Group
LONDON AND NEW YORK

First published 2023
by Routledge
4 Park Square, Milton Park, Abingdon, Oxon OX14 4RN

and by Routledge
605 Third Avenue, New York, NY 10158

Routledge is an imprint of the Taylor & Francis Group, an informa business

British Library Cataloguing-in-Publication Data
A catalogue record for this book is available from the British Library

Library of Congress Cataloging-in-Publication Data
Names: Brito, Cleiton Maciel, author.
Title: China and globalization in the Amazon : workers, expatriates and the Chinese production model / Cleiton Maciel Brito.
Description: Abingdon, Oxon ; New York, NY : Routledge, 2023. | Series: Global connections | Includes bibliographical references and index.
Identifiers: LCCN 2022033822 (print) | LCCN 2022033823 (ebook) | ISBN 9781032127156 (hbk) | ISBN 9781032134727 (pbk) | ISBN 9781003229377 (ebk)
Subjects: LCSH: Investments, Chinese—Brazil—Amazon River Region. | Industrial relations—Brazil—Amazon River Region. | Industrial management—Brazil—Amazon River Region. | Globalization—Brazil—Amazon River Region.
Classification: LCC HG5340.A4 B57 2023 (print) | LCC HG5340.A4 (ebook) | DDC 332.60951—dc23/eng/20220923
LC record available at https://lccn.loc.gov/2022033822
LC ebook record available at https://lccn.loc.gov/2022033823

ISBN: 978-1-032-12715-6 (hbk)
ISBN: 978-1-032-13472-7 (pbk)
ISBN: 978-1-003-22937-7 (ebk)

DOI: 10.4324/9781003229377

Typeset in Bembo
by Apex CoVantage, LLC

To Jeanne, Natanael, and Melissa, a lifetime love.

CONTENTS

GRAPHICS

TABLES

FIGURES

PREFACE

The city of Manaus, in the Brazilian state of Amazonas, is the largest city in northern Brazil with a population of 2,600,000,000 in its metropolitan area (data from 2018). It is located in the inlands of the Brazilian Amazon, surrounded by the rainforest and large rivers such as the Negro and the Amazonas/Solimões. It has almost no access by road to the rest of the country and rivers have replaced highways, as a means of transport for products and people, leaving air transport as the only way to overcome the long distances of a continental country in less time, which is fundamental for its economic activities.

Despite its geographical isolation, its population has grown continuously, as has its industrial activity, becoming one of the richest Brazilian metropolises and one of the most unequal, which reflects the historical inequality present in our society. Although surrounded by water, it has problems with water supply and basic sanitation that only serves 25% of its population, aggravated by the existing poverty in its outskirts and in the stilt houses located on the rivers. Manaus is not the only city with such problems; it shares with other northern and northeastern cities the lowest HDI indexes in the country.

Manaus is a Free Trade Zone, with generous tax incentives – reduced taxes and lower import duties – offered by the federal, state, and municipal governments, as a means to attract national and foreign investments. Starting in the late 1960s, it became a large market for cheap imported products, which in many cases offset the long trips. The Industrial Center was also created, attracting companies in the electro-electronic and two-wheeler (motorcycle) sectors. The economic dynamism resulting from the installation of numerous factories did not result in investments in the city's infrastructure and, consequently, in its population's quality of life. However, more than 50 years later, it has not created an industrialization process in the region, becoming more and more dependent on imported inputs, especially with the rise of China.

The research conducted by Cleiton Maciel, using Manaus as a reference, is distinguished by its originality by bringing together two themes so far little investigated: the industrial sector in the city of Manaus and the arrival of Chinese companies, starting in the 2000s, with more than 20 factories installed, their distinct work culture, the influx of Chinese workers, and the "expatriate workers". The author analyses this new moment as a "Chinese model of production", making an analogy to the "Japanese model" – this one is widely analyzed by the sociological and organizational literature.

The research covered Chinese companies and their forms of organization, workers, labor union members, and government employees involved in the Manaus Industrial Park. In all of them, the concern was to recover, among those different players, their perceptions on how production is organized. Cleiton Maciel conducted observations of work carried out in four factories, interviewing both Chinese and Brazilian workers and comparing Brazilian with Chinese labor legislations, as a means to understand the distinct forms of work culture in the two countries, pointing out that Brazilian workers, as long as they have had formal jobs, they would have more rights. The author also emphasizes the Chinese management's lack of understanding concerning these rights and their attempts to adapt to the country's norms, sometimes with little success. Still, he did not find a "bloody Taylorism" or "slave labor" as Chinese capital was portrayed nationally, even though it always remained at the limit of legislation, without any extra benefits for the worker.

Cleiton Maciel uses a vast bibliography, describing recent changes in China, its economic dynamism, labor regulation, and the expansion of Chinese capital abroad as a strategy to strengthen its own industry and economy. In other terms, he analyzes China's advance as a global economic power, with diversified investments all over the world. However, unlike Chinese investment in Africa, the research shows the almost nonexistence of a greater concern for political and cultural insertion, despite the facts that the two countries are joint participants in the BRICS and China is Brazil's largest trading partner. He presents the prejudices disseminated in Brazil about China, reported by the interviewees who largely repeat the US narrative of the Asian threat.

During the research procedures, Cleiton Maciel reveals the difficulties of access to Chinese workers, which was partially solved with the use of "Guanxi", a characteristic of Chinese sociability, necessary to establish trust among peers and widely used in business transactions. Some of the findings of these interviews are the wages paid to Chinese workers at the factories in Manaus, including supervisory or managerial positions, which were lower than those paid to Brazilian workers, something unusual in Brazil.

The use of expatriate workers by the companies' headquarters is a form to control production and implementation of a "Chinese model", whose main characteristics are what the author calls "matrix Taylorism", which excludes the participation of workers in the day-to-day management of the factory floor, thus maintaining rigidity and distance from the workers. In this case, comparison is made with other foreign companies in the industrial complex, which the workers see as more inclined to meet their demands. It also highlights that the "expatriation of workers" by China functions as a kind of internship and the possibility of advancement upon return to China, a situation strongly desired by expatriates.

A curiosity pointed out was the Chinese management's practice, at the beginning of the activities in Manaus, to yell at production workers, leading the Human Resources sectors to offer good manners course to the newcomers to adapt to the local habits. This does not mean that this behavior does not exist in Brazilian and other multinational companies. In any case, the arrival of Chinese factories and workers illustrates the foreign nature of two business cultures in their relations with workers and how workers react to the slow "normalization" process of these companies in the country, which implicates the observation of not only Brazilian legislation but also a distinct labor culture.

The book, which is a result of Cleiton Maciel's doctoral thesis, presents a deep and high-quality research in which the author has invested heavily. The originality of the research earned the author an "honorable mention" from CAPES (a Ministry of Education agency that evaluates and regulates graduate studies) for the best thesis defended in 2018 in Brazil.

Therefore, it is a deep and refined research, with a sociological eye on Brazilian emerging social issues and on Brazil's insertion "from below" in global capitalism.

São Carlos, May 2022

Jacob Carlos Lima
President of the Brazilian Sociological Association
Professor of the Department of Sociology
Federal University of São Carlos

ACKNOWLEDGMENTS

For a person born and raised along Amazon riverside in the middle of the jungle surrounded by rivers and forests and who managed to graduate from university, this book has a special meaning: the search for knowledge and the struggles before the "Amazonian difficulties" were worthwhile. It also means a feeling of satisfaction and happiness to be able to contribute to social science in this part of the world, where nature and culture meet challenging our understanding and that has increasingly become a global issue.

During this trajectory, countless people helped make this path less uncertain, more welcoming, and encouraged every step I took, from my human formation as a farmer and riverbank dweller to the first years of research in social sciences, until the final elaboration of this book. To them, I here give my most sincere acknowledgments.

First of all, I would like to thank my parents, Mr. João Pereira Maciel, a migrant rubber tapper and Amazonian farmer, and Mrs. Terezinha Maciel, who initiated me into reading, as a child. Both of them have always been the reason why I wanted to achieve so much, as well as an inspiration in life, struggle, and resistance. Through them, I also thank the entire Maciel family, especially my siblings, Tatiana, Sérgio, Carlos Henrique, Carlos Alexandre, and Taina and my niece, Dhécika, who helped me with the transcription of the interviews.

It would not be possible to write this book without a warm home and a safe harbor. It is easier to do science with feelings. Jeanne Brito Maciel, my wife, also a PhD in sociology, was an emotional support and intellectual friend, as well as an inexhaustible source of love and affection. She participated in most of the field research as my "assistant", helped me with the reading of the manuscripts, and made several comments that made the text more concise, cohesive, and with more analytical rigor. My son, Natanael, was understanding, friendly, and patient when he just wanted to play. He always asked me, "Dad, when are you going to finish this book about China?" It is ready, Nanan. Shall we play?

Professor Jacob Carlos Lima, of the Department of Sociology of the Federal University of São Carlos and President of the Brazilian Sociological Society, was my doctoral advisor and an exemplary intellectual. Advising me patiently and seriously, he corrected directions, indicated paths, and showed me possibilities and challenges. I also owe him for the indications as to how to transform the research into text and for the recommendation of countless bibliographies, both essential to the theoretical debate in this volume. I am also grateful to him for accepting my invitation and honoring me with the preface to this book.

My introduction to sociology of labor and globalization would not be possible without the inspiration and guidance of Izabel Valle, a professor at the Federal University of Amazonas and an intellectual who mentored me during my first field researches in the Amazon and who read and commented on the manuscript. Marcelo Seráfico, also from the Federal University of Amazonas, provided me with many theoretical insights about capitalism in its "low circuits" and in the emerging economies context. These teachers had great influence in the text. I hope I expressed well this good influence.

I am grateful to José Fernandes and Valdenízia Oliveira for hosting me for several months while I conducted my field research in the city of Manaus. They are friends and as the parents that I gained in life. They welcomed me as their son with great generosity. It is a very dear family, especially Jônatas and Victor, friends in leisure time and otherwise, who, as a computer scientist and engineer, made me enjoy "data" and discover forms to understand many of the quantitative aspects of research. They also gave me the benefit of hearing my doubts and reading my comments and parts of this manuscript. I am grateful to you, brothers.

I would like to thank the Graduate Program in Sociology at the Federal University of São Carlos, the public university where I received my PhD in Sociology, for the hospitality, teaching, and academic structure necessary for this research. To my fellow professors, Marcelo Seraphic, Izabel Valle, Alessandra Rachid, and Aline Pires, I am indebted for their careful and critical readings of the first drafts of this manuscript.

I am indebted to many colleagues who, during the field research in Manaus, opened the doors of factories, unions, employers' institutions, and agencies within the Manaus Free Trade Zone. I could not forget to mention Farid Mendonça, Marluce Carvalho, Abelardo Costa, Edilon, and Henrique. In addition to them, I must register my gratitude to the factory workers who were very kind to grant interviews and describe to me part of their daily work, many times in their own homes. Their accounts enriched the research and made the local understanding of Global China more detailed and empirical.

I thank the Chinese expatriates for sharing information concerning their work in China and the Manaus Free Trade Zone. Of these, my special thanks go to Mila Yang, André Shang, Roger Nang, and Marcos Lee. Through their friendship and the story of their journeys, they helped me learn about essential aspects of Chinese culture and the mobility of expatriate workers that emerges with the rise of Global China.

In dealing with a research intended to point out the origin and expansion of a Chinese model of production, the theoretical dialogue with the international literature was fundamental. In this respect, I must mention the bibliographical assistance of Chris Smith, of the Royal Holloway University of London, and Mingwei Liu, of Rutgers University. I am extremely grateful for sharing their writings on Chinese factory labor globalization, especially in the European context and in Mainland China.

I am extremely grateful to Raimundo Moura for translating the entire text into English. His suggestions for translation and vocabulary corrections were very important. Thank you for accepting the task of making the Amazonian culture and language more understandable to non-Portuguese speakers.

I owe special thanks to Neil Jordan for making this book possible. I am grateful for his patience with the deadlines, his comments about the book's structure, and his generosity in promptly responding to all the questions and requests I submitted to him.

Finally, I thank the Foundation for Research Support of the State of Amazonas (FAPEAM), for awarding me a four-year research grant, which allowed me to study in a different state of the country, dedicate full time to academic activities, and conduct field studies in the factories in Manaus. I wish many other people would have the privilege of studying the Brazilian reality and, with full support from the government and private sector for the development of national science, help to build a fair and happy Brazil.

ABBREVIATIONS

ACFTU – All-China Federation of Trade Unions
BRI – Belt and Road Initiative
BRICS – Brazil, Russia, India, China and South Africa
CBERS – China–Brazil Earth Resources Satellite
CCP – Chinese Communist Party
CIEAM – Center of Industries of the State of Amazonas
CKD – Completely Knocked Down
FIEAM – Federation of Industries of the State of Amazonas
GDP – Gross Domestic Product
CSIG – China South Industries Group
HR – Human Resources
II – Import Tax
ILO – International Labor Organization
IPI – Tax on Industrialized Products
MDIC – Ministry of Development, Industry and Foreign Trade
NPI – New Product Introduction
PCB – Printed Circuit Board
PIM – Manaus Industrial Park
PPB – Basic Productive Process
SEZs – Special Economic Zones
SOE – State-Owned Enterprise
SUFRAMA – Superintendence of the Manaus Free Trade Zone
TBO – Basic Operational Training
ZFM – Manaus Free Trade Zone

1

INTRODUCTION

The Chinese globalization and the new silk road in the Amazon

The Manaus city and its savage global factories

Over the past few years, the world has observed a rapid rush to form "little Chinas" around the globe (Lima & Valle 2013) and no region has escaped the clutches of the Asian dragon. Europe and Asia, for example, have been arenas for intense Chinese capital advance and China's strategy of connection and mobility, as shown by Gao (2004), Meunier (2012), Burgoon & Raess (2014), Andrijasevic & Sacchetto (2016), and Smith & Zheng (2016).

But it is the southern hemisphere that concentrates one of the main waves of China's action in the world, especially in Africa and South America. Search for copper and infrastructure construction in countries like Zambia and Tanzania has led authors to characterize the Chinese presence in the region as "enclaves" (Lee 2009), as comprehensive accumulation and accumulation by maximization (Lee 2017), or to investigate whether China would be promoting a new colonization process on the continent (Hung 2018; Bodomo 2019). Other authors have been describing Chinese presence in various countries through financing and loans (Burlamaqui 2015) or via "infrastructure diplomacy" (Cintra & Pinto 2017).

In terms of South America, Brazil stands out as the leading destination for Chinese investments in the region,[1] focusing mainly on mining, energy (Tang 2017), oil and gas (Hung 2018), infrastructure (Nascimento & Maynetto 2019), agribusiness sector (Escher & Wilkinson 2019), 5G technology (Saraiva & Silva 2019), and participation in the Brazilian industrial and production park (Maciel Brito 2017).

These are the sectors where the Chinese have been concentrating their investments in Brazil, especially the oil and gas located along the Brazilian coast.

However, when the oil and gas sector is excluded, a peculiar region emerges as a new route for Chinese actions in Brazil. We are talking about the Amazon.

DOI: 10.4324/9781003229377-1

Beginning in the nineteenth century, Amazon has been a space of capitalist economic globalization. However, not until the twentieth century that capitalism advanced significantly in the region. An example is the emergence in Manaus[2] – the main Amazonian city – of an industrial region resulting from transformations of capitalism in Brazil: Manaus Free Trade Zone (ZFM in Portuguese).

ZFM was created on February 28, 1967, by the Brazilian military government.[3] ZFM is one of the first free trade zones implemented in the world and represents a combination of diverse interests, both national and global.

At the international level, it responded to capitalist desire to create new markets and new world consumers, in a period when several countries were protecting their own internal markets. It also aimed to streamline and adjust capital, by relieving it from labor union pressures and labor costs in developed countries.

At the national level, the Brazilian military dictatorship saw with good eyes opening part of the national territory to global capital, while keeping other regions "closed" (Silva 2013). It attracted international capital, but "protected" the Brazilian companies located mainly in southern and southeastern Brazil. Coupled to this, there was the debate over what to do with the Amazon, seen by the Brazilian military as a target of international greed.

In the regional scenario, the Amazon's economy was stagnant and based mainly on forest product extraction. Moreover, the local elite of Manaus felt that it had been neglected, which was explained by the fact that the region had experienced national and even international prominence in the late nineteenth and early twentieth centuries, a time when rubber extracted from rubber trees accounted for almost 50% of Brazil's total exports. Therefore, the ZFM surges as a kind of political and economic "redemption" for the local economy (Seráfico 2011).

It was before this scenario that the Amazon region became ZFM home, whose main "competitive advantage" was a tax policy differentiated from the rest of the country, based on tax and nontax incentives to the projects installed in this special economic zone.[4] That was consistent with global capital interests, which sought to circumvent both labor and tax costs of national states. The local elite found it valid, because it would lower the "Amazonian costs".[5]

According to the project which created the ZFM, it would consist of the development of a commercial, agricultural, and industrial pole.[6] However, only the commercial/industrial centers became a reality, especially the latter, which became known as the Manaus Industrial Park (PIM).[7] Since then, PIM has been the location for the most diverse factories from many different industrial sectors and many different parts of the world.

This can be observed, for example, when one indicates that in the 1970s and 1980s, PIM was dominated by North American, European, and Japanese capital investment. Back then, labor had a strong hierarchical content, with no worker participation, low qualification, and simple tasks execution. That was when unions emerged and capital was strongly contested.

Then, in the 1990s, the "Asian Tigers" arrived, especially South Korean companies, setting a new investment cycle. During this period, the Japanese management model became the production standard, whose main pillars were "participative management", "just in time", "quality culture", "collaboration", "worker skills", and the "multiskilled and multifunctional worker". There was also greater local participation in the elaboration of industrial processes of global companies.

This is when a certain "standard" for national and local labor was established, which, under union pressure, resulted in labor benefits and profit sharing. As a managerial expression, policies of worker involvement and concession of awards and recognition to workers were consolidated in order to dissuade them from labor unions and increase productivity. Valle (2007) called this process as *neolaylorism*, given the combination of workers' nonparticipation and production flexibility. Oliveira (2007) characterizes it as a "new productive pattern".

Starting in the 2000s, a new investment matrix emerged in Manaus: China. In concrete terms, more than 20 state-owned, semi-state-owned, and private factories arrived in Manaus, which by 2014 accounted for almost 10% of the total number of PIM employees.

The arrival of these Chinese companies made it necessary to learn how this impacted labor in Brazil. First of all, it was absolutely needed to understand what this new player was up to in the Amazon, how they were received, how they related to local agents, and how they dealt with Brazilian workers. Second, due to a surge of research on Chinese factories around the world, indicating distinct and diverse work models, such as "bloody Taylorism", "managerial despotism", "Trojan horses", and "Chinese enclaves", what would be the behavior of these factories on Brazilian soil?

In addition, many complaints arose from the factory floor in Brazil, mainly coming from the labor unions. Among them, the Chinese factories were violating Brazilian labor laws and it would be better if they left the country. And, finally, opinion polls[8] indicated that 42% of the Chinese companies' employees installed in Brazil resigned from these companies during their first year of employment, which represented a turnover rate 68% higher when compared to those of European or American companies.

This process went in the opposite direction of what researches done in Brazil in the 1990s indicated, emphasizing the Japanese managerial tricks. Therefore, which Chinese form of work was implemented in Manaus? And how would this impact local workers, particularly in a context of managerial culture, until then, dominated by the so-called "Japanese model" of organizing capitalist production, supposedly with greater worker participation?

Between tambaqui[9] and soups: on how (not) to do ethnography in Chinese factories

It was in this context of China's global expansion and changes in the labor world that, between July 2013 and March 2017, I conducted sociological research in four Chinese factories installed in the Manaus Industrial Park: a) a privately owned electronic board factory (China Board[10]); b) a privately owned television, notebook, and tablet factory (TVChina); c) a state-owned motorcycle factory (MotorChina); and d) a semi-state-owned air-conditioning factory (ArconChina).

To get to these companies, I selected the main productive sectors, the most representative Chinese companies in each sector, and, among those, the ones that fell into the categories of the period they had been installed in PIM: long, medium, and short. This choice was fundamental to encompass both changes and permanence of the Chinese processes, as well as to indicate what was new and already structured in Manaus.

In the research, I used a triangulation of methods, both qualitative and quantitative: analysis of documentary sources (in Portuguese and English) and financial data from PIM companies, use of dense description (Geertz 1973), of anthropological observation, participant observation (Cardoso 2000), and labor ethnography (Pun 2005; Lee 2017). I also interviewed workers, union leaders, business leaders, public managers, labor court prosecutors, Brazilian managers, and Chinese expatriates who held various positions in companies.

The focus was to comprehensively address the various aspects and social players involved with the factories under investigation: from commodity and production process to feelings, immaterial goods, and social identities (Bourdieu 1977; Appadurai 1996; Hall 1992; Gaetano 2015), while maintaining methodological distance in a social space context familiar to the researcher (Velho 1981).

Using the "snowball" strategy, meaning that each individual indicated another colleague, I interviewed male and female workers from the companies' most diverse hierarchical levels, especially those from the factory floor, until repetition of the answers was achieved, as advocated by Gondim & Lima (2006).

The problem was that sometimes the snowball almost collapsed, because many female workers contacted were afraid of scheduling interviews with a male interlocutor. As a result, in terms of methodology, the search for interviews with female workers at PIM began to be conducted by my research assistant; with regard to workers, by me, a strategy that was fundamental and made the interview wheel turn again.

I also made annual visits to the plants to follow the production process and obtain socioeconomic data from the companies. The research at the factories was obtained through different means. Initially, I contacted the companies by phone and e-mail, but didn't have any positive response. I also tried through work ethnography, being part of the workforce in one of the factories investigated. After being approved by the Brazilian management, my entry was blocked by the Chinese headquarters.

At the same time, I approached business, government, and labor union institutions operating in the Manaus Free Trade Zone. In television and plate factories, for example, access occurred under union referral, because the union leaders had close contact with Human Resources managers of these companies, who were Brazilians. In the air-conditioning factory, the access was through a referral from an official from the Superintendence of the Manaus Free Trade Zone (SUFRAMA)[11] who, coincidentally, had been a graduate student of my doctoral advisor. Finally, the Center of Industries of the State of Amazonas (CIEAM)[12] introduced me to the motorcycle factory. From then on, the contacts made with factory managers led to subsequent visits.

In addition to interviews with workers and direct observation of the companies' production processes, it was necessary to conduct research among those who were a key part of the Chinese factories installed in the Amazon – the expatriates transferred from China to Manaus. Their relevance to the research had already become clear during the first conversations I had with Brazilian labor union representatives, who spoke about "Chinese missions" holding the highest positions in the factories and "fiercely controlling the workers".

At the international level, some authors, such as Lee (2009), Cooke (2012), and Smith & Zheng (2016), observed the prominence of expatriates in factories in Tanzania, Zambia, India, and Turkey. However, there were no data on Chinese factories and expatriates at the South American level. Therefore, the question that emerged was whether this was really occurring in Brazil, and if so, its modes of local operation, on the one hand, and its general aspects when compared to the rest of the world, on the other.

Corroborating this global trend, when the research began in mid-2013, one of the first aspects that caught my attention was exactly this: Chinese permeating the entire management and supervisory organization of these companies, even among those who have been in the Amazon for quite some time. Therefore, there was a starting point for further investigation, which led me to map out who these individuals were and what their social function was in the researched factories.

However, it became clear from the very beginning of the research that obtaining data on expatriates would be no easy task. They were suspicious and controlled basic information about the factory and about themselves. During the interviews scheduled by the Brazilian management and conducted inside the companies, little information was formally obtained, with only their name, age, and positions in the organization being provided. It was necessary to change the strategy to move ahead with the research.

In this search for a dense description (Geertz 1973), the strategy was to make the interviews less formal, so that the Chinese would feel more comfortable about answering the research questions. Therefore, I invited them to go out and talk to me in restaurants in the city of Manaus. Some of them alleged commitments and denied, but other expats accepted the invitation. In the restaurants, between tambaqui and soups (dishes that they enjoyed a lot), I sought out more details about their lives as expats.[13]

However, despite the good food and the fact that they never allowed me and my assistant to pay for any of the bills, the information we were looking for simply did not turn up. When we asked a more complex question, we heard a short answer with no depth, under suspicious glances, and with comments among themselves in Mandarin.

In fact, at the beginning, I was interviewed more than I interviewed. The Chinese wanted to know everything: why I was doing that research, how the university functioned in Brazil, what I would do after I finished my doctorate, how much I was paid and how much I would receive as a future professor, what was the Brazilian political system, and what I anticipated about the "economic trends of the country", among other things. What I did not know was that this was part of the research process among the Chinese. Gaetano (2015), Lee (2009, 2017), and Pinheiro-Machado (2011, 2017), for example, went through similar situations and used local strategies and contexts to enter the Chinese world. They made "Guanxi".[14]

I was doing it too, but still in a very formal sense, combining leisure time with work, without much success. Even my clothes were still "academic", as I wore a shirt and "social" pants. Not only that, but my own way of conducting the conversations, using notebooks and pens, trying to write down everything they said, scared the expatriates away, or at least inhibited them. To make matters worse, I sometimes asked if I could record the dialogues. Afraid, they would not allow it, and I, feeling that I was not advancing, was running out of interviews and data.

Only after these "Amazonian difficulties", I did change the way I was conducting Guanxi and things started to move. Instead of formalities, I started to use local charms in an attempt to approach the Chinese. One of them consisted in inviting them to go fishing at a family ranch, located in the interior of the Amazon. Another consisted in always bringing them some regional gift during the meetings.

In addition, inviting them to my house in Manaus was an important strategy (mutual trust). That was an attraction and a new universe for them, so they wanted to see all the rooms of the house and know how much it would cost to rent a place like that. Furthermore, having a "big" house in a metropolis like Manaus showed them "my social ascension".[15] Bringing them into our world was a sign of respect and consideration.

Therefore, it is in this context that the course of our conversations moved from a formal meaning toward "China business". During these negotiations, my recommendations came to be appreciated and valued. One example is that the Chinese asked my opinion about the most important Amazonian medicinal products, since they intended to take them to sell in China; they also asked about which investments in the Amazon would bring good financial returns. Buying land, planting açaí or guaraná trees, and raising fish were the things that they were especially interested in. "In some of these businesses", they said enthusiastically, "you will become our partner in the future, when you finish your doctorate".

I never really knew if they meant it or not, but the important thing is that trust was gradually being built and the world of the expatriate being opened up to me. It is important to point out that signs of this trust came even before the data itself. For example, they began to bring me gifts on their return from their annual trips to China and invite me to visit their country. They also gave me their personal contacts from their messaging application, which permitted me, even when I was far away, to exchange information and address some issues that arose later.

In addition, they began to receive me in their dormitories in the city of Manaus to eat Chinese food that they had cooked themselves. Too spicy, even for Amazonian standards, and especially for a researcher inexperienced in Chinese cuisine, the "rice bowl" offered by the expatriates in their own residences was the material and symbolic proof that the Guanxi relationship was effectively materialized and that I could, from then on, take care of the "academic business", moving into other directions in the data collection.

Therefore, that is how, after many comings and goings, trial and error on how to conduct the conversations and, mainly, on how to learn not to ask, but to talk and listen, I entered the physical and symbolic universe of the expatriates. I say this because doing Guanxi required persistence, time, and an exchange of goods (material and immaterial), without knowing, afterward, who was receiving more or less information, because the important thing was the interchange.

The most sensitive information, such as salaries, benefits, social trajectory, routines, fears, and expats' plans, were obtained thanks to this methodological strategy.

Chinese factories: the need to exorcise the ghost

The process of Chinese factories' arrival in the Amazon – to use a classic expression of Karl Marx – has not ceased to be a "specter" haunting the region. I say this by referring to the way many Amazonian agents – unionists, business leaders, and public administrators – interpreted the Chinese arrival, using a chain of representation about the Chinese ascension and expansion throughout the world, and more specifically in the Amazon.

Among these concepts, some claimed that it was the arrival of the "communist dictatorship" or "slaves sent by the Chinese government". Others said that China needed to "export millions of starving people" to other countries. Others saw the investments with good eyes, but were suspicious that the Chinese did not create any technology locally, but only imported and assembled their goods in Manaus.

Such rumors about the Chinese are not unique to the Amazon and they are diverse. Lee (2017), for example, observed narratives in Zambia, Africa. The author shows how a local negative imagery about the Chinese has been triggered by the Chinese themselves to become part of their narratives that identifies them as "secular victims of the West". In Europe, some authors will refer to Chinese investment as a "Trojan Horse".

This type of vision has received even more impetus with the pandemic caused by the new Coronavirus and many have used this opportunity to create the idea of a "Chinese virus". All in all, we have before us different forms of accusing China and surrounding it from all sides, whether in the geopolitical and economic or labor issues, even in matters of health. According to these perceptions, Chinese globalization is spreading evil all over the planet.

In fact, as Hairong & Sautman (2012) have already pointed out, this is a quest to demonize China, "without evidence", something that is part of the new global ideological dispute and political and economic rivalry over contracts or geostrategic issues.

Given this global game about what Chinese expansion really is, this research seeks to contribute sociologically by indicating the impacts of Chinese factories on workers in the Amazon. Through an ethnography among the various players involved in this process, and via analysis of economic and social data, the central issue consisted in investigating the local labor world before the arrival of global Chinese factories, observing transformations, continuities, and the speech of those involved, but separating the wheat from the chaff.

Structure of the book

The basic structure of this volume relies on the argument that a Chinese production model is emerging with industrial and managerial characteristics that have caused major changes in the type of work visualized until then. The book aims to contribute to Global China studies, to labor and organizational sociology, and to the debate concerning the Amazon's place in the new scenario of the global economy. To present this line of reasoning, the book is organized into six chapters, starting with this introductory Chapter 1, which shows the major issues of the research and its methodological aspects, and summarizes how my field research took place in the Chinese factories in the Amazon.

In Chapter 2, the central issue addresses the rise of global China focusing on three dimensions: economic reforms, labor reforms, and changes in worker management. To this end, I address the set of economic and social transformations that China has undergone since the late 1970s. Then, I address the metamorphoses in labor relations, emphasizing migrant labor and labor legislation reforms. Besides helping to explain the Chinese development, it will be fundamental to associate it with the Chinese workers' view of the Brazilian labor laws. In the last part of the chapter, I do a literature survey on the main aspects of labor management in both China and outside it, emphasizing its elements in Europe and Africa.

Chapter 3 discusses how Chinese globalization occurred at the Manaus Industrial Park and presents the organizational elements of the Chinese Model of Production (CMP). I initiate by highlighting the economic and political aspects of the China–Brazil relationship, focusing on the two countries' main interests over the years, and present an overview of the Chinese advance in several areas of the Brazilian economy. I also address the arrival of Chinese investments in the Amazon as part of a new Chinese route that involves geopolitical, economic, and industrial interests. Afterward, I characterize the installation of the factories in Manaus, emphasizing their acceptance by the local economic and union leaderships. I also trace their organizational profiles and argue that the Human Resources system of these companies functions as a Chinese enclave, without local autonomy. Finally, I point out the import of almost all the inputs used in production from China as a basic characteristic of the Chinese model, in an attempt to control not only the production chain but also the export of raw materials on a global level.

Chapter 4 discusses the managerial characteristics of the Chinese production model and its impacts on the workers in Manaus. I initially discuss the profile of the workers surveyed and identify the construction of strong and weak bonds between them, with emphasis on the relationship with the unions and the formation of their identities and trajectories at the Manaus Industrial Park. Then, I highlight these companies' management policies, focusing on their impacts on workers in terms of wages, benefits, involvement, worker participation, professional qualifications, and opportunities for professional growth. Finally, I characterize the changes and permanence in the factory work process, describing the Chinese particularities. The chapter's final issue concludes that the investigated factories promoted a precarious work in Manaus, without creating strong bonds with the city, by creating a heavy factory, with inflexible, technical, bureaucratic, routine, nonparticipative management, and strongly linked to China, what configures a *matrix Taylorism*.

Chapter 5 discusses the role of expatriation in the current expansion of Chinese factories. To that end, I provide a theoretical survey of this social phenomenon, showing that it has been a consistent mechanism of workers and capital mobility in the globalization promoted by China. Through interviews and interaction with Chinese expatriates in Manaus, I retrace their trajectories, describing their journeys from rural China to working in Amazon factories. Furthermore, I show the Chinese expatriation peculiarities in relation to the other companies present in Manaus and their benefits for the headquarters, such as wage costs, labor control, and asceticism that mixes moral commitment with the Chinese economic need. I call this process *disciplined expatriation*, a conjunction of matrix control with the expatriate's self-discipline and agency. I also outline how local workers interpret and relate to this system, describing their dissatisfactions and scoring what they see as the Chinese's privileges over other local workers.

The concluding chapter reflects the significance of the book to understand the current stage of Chinese globalization and the role of the Amazon in the local/global relationship. To this end, I summarize the arguments made throughout the chapters and highlight how the Chinese model borrows many of the Western production practices, but introduces original elements. By emphasizing the key ones, I conclude the book with the assertion that besides the investment of capital, Global China also implies a production model with some basic characteristics disseminated and coordinated worldwide. Hence, the necessity for new empirical studies that map the unfolding, in diverse contexts, of Chinese managerial and industrial practices, revealing more elements and characteristics of a Chinese model of production with a global dimension.

Notes

1 In 2017, the Brazil received around 50% of Chinese investments in South America.
2 Manaus is the capital of the state of Amazonas, being one of the main cities in Brazil, both in terms of population (2.1 million inhabitants) and in economy (among the Brazilian capitals, it is the 8th Gross Domestic Product). It is also known for being located in the region with the greatest biodiversity on the planet: the Amazon.
3 Originally scheduled to end in 1997, ZFM has been extended four times. Currently, the termination date set by law is 2073.
4 Some of the fiscal incentives granted are import tax (II) reduction of up to 88% on inputs for industrialization; exemption from Tax on Industrialized Products (IPI.); 75% reduction in Corporate Income Tax; and plots of land at a symbolic price.

5 Lack of highways or railroads connecting the region with the rest of the country and the distance from its main consumer market: the São Paulo region.
6 The commercial pole was prominent up until the early 1990s, when the opening of Brazil's trade took away the comparative advantage of trade in the ZFM. The agricultural pole has never been effectively developed. The industrial pole began to grow in the mid-1970s, and it is the one that stands out until today.
7 PIM closed the year 2021 with more than 500 companies installed, providing direct jobs to more than 100 thousand workers.
8 For more information: https://www1.folha.uol.com.br/fsp/mercado/me0805201104.htm.
9 One of the most appreciated fish in the Amazon, both by locals and by tourists.
10 The company names are fictitious.
11 SUFRAMA is a Public Administration agency affiliated to the Ministry of Development, Industry and Foreign Trade (MDIC) of Brazil. It manages and controls the fiscal incentives granted to the companies established in the Manaus Free Trade Zone, besides promoting development strategies for Western Amazon.
12 An employer entity.
13 In general, the interviews were conducted in Portuguese, but at times, they were also held in English. Translation limits were circumvented by constant repetition of interviews and the creation of bonds with the interviewees.
14 The term refers to special relationships whose main bases are a continual exchange of favors, loyalty, moral leadership, the flow of trust, the spirit of harmony, hierarchy among different people, and the obligation of bonds. "Two people enjoying a *guanxi* relationship can assume that each is conscientiously committed to the other" (Chen 2004: 45).
15 According to them, a large house would be impossible to buy in China because "the price was too high for someone with an average income" under the Chinese real estate boom.

2

FROM MAO TO A NEW DAWN? FUNDAMENTALS OF CHINESE GLOBALIZATION AT HOME AND ABROAD

Crisis of Mao Zedong's period and Chinese economic reforms

After the Chinese Communist Party (CCP) gained power in 1949, overthrowing the Nationalist Party[1] government, Mao Zedong began a process of reforming all laws and policies implemented by the former government and formulating a political system based on socialist principles. This policy's main objectives were based on the transformation of the workers as the main subjects of the productive process, being considered the "masters of the Chinese factories".

The *Labor Insurance Regulations* promulgated in 1951 had as one of its main elements the universal lifelong employment model, where workers could enjoy job security because the law provided lifetime employment. This process is called the Iron Rice Bowl, because it offered workers a range of benefits such as pensions, housing, health care, and schooling in the *work unit*.[2] In addition, workers' wage levels were not set by company management, but by Communist Party members.

Even though lifetime employment and the work unit system were considered the keys to Mao's rule, according to Jianzhou (2006), this system led to an excess of labor in industry, and did not provide workers with productive incentives, therefore low productivity in State-Owned Enterprises.

Theorists from the Communist Party's more liberal wing believed that production models based on universal lifetime employment had exhausted the state enterprises' efficiency: they "ate from the pot" of the Communist state and workers "ate from the pot" of the state enterprises, leaving no room for creativity, production optimization, and enthusiasm on the part of the workers.

The first attempt to change Mao Zedong's labor policy was set against the high unemployment level that swept China in the late 1970s and early 1980s. This level of unemployment was associated with population growth, especially among the

DOI: 10.4324/9781003229377-2

urban population as thousands of individuals who had been sent back to rural villages during the Cultural Revolution returned to the cities.

The return of this large contingent put pressure on the government, which increased government capital investment, built new factories, and forced state-owned companies to accommodate the returns from rural areas, a situation that became known as "five people doing the job of three". Furthermore, it introduced the so-called "dingti" (occupational inheritance), meaning that a retired worker could let his or her child take up his or her job.

These CCP measures caused the government to employ a percentage of workers beyond the actual capacity of the state-owned companies, worsening China's economic situation.

Therefore, the post-Mao leaders, based on the Communist Party general secretary Deng Xiaoping's ideas – who proclaimed that "*to get rich is glorious*" – initiated a series of reforms in China's economy that would lead to "socialism with Chinese characteristics" and would turn China into the "factory of the world" (Zhang 2006).

Thus, with Mao Zedong's death in 1976 and the crisis in China's productive sector, Deng Xiaoping began to lead the country by introducing "four modernizations": agriculture, industry, defense, and science and technology. Deng's idea was to first enrich some regions and then, based on what he learned, enrich other parts of the country (Jabbour 2012).

In terms of agriculture, Deng reformed the land grant system. From 1979 onward, the people's communes were no longer in force, it was replaced by the contract that made the families responsible for the business. Under this system, they divided the land among families, who could exploit the area over a period of 15 years.[3] Unlike the reform promoted by Mao, this one permitted any production surplus to be sold in the market, creating an "enthusiasm" in the rural population, which summarized the system with the following saying: "Provide what is necessary to the State, give enough to the collective, and the rest for yourselves" (Guoyng 2004).

Accordingly, Deng Xiaoping reestablished the pact between the State and the peasant class, by promoting the institutionalization of individual accumulation among peasants. By being able to save part of their production for themselves, peasants started to plan the production process, which also counted on State's participation in the technological improvement, making agriculture technological, more irrigated areas, increasing the production and the consumption of fertilizers, and promoting rural area electrification in China. In addition, the families were allowed to hire up to seven workers per family, creating rural wage in agriculture. In addition to this, the advent of the one-child[4] policy resulted in more planning among Chinese rural families.

As a result, China's cereal production grew from 277 million tons in 1980 to 400 million tons in 1990 (China Statistical Yearbook 2004 *apud* Jabbour 2010), 405 million tons in 2000, and over 500 million tons as of 2012. China became one of the largest cereal producers in the world, despite having only 121 million hectares of farmland suitable for cultivation.[5] From grain importer, China began to export it, by aggregating value to it. Consequently, the agricultural participation in the GDP increased 2,456 times in relation to 1978, a gradual growth rate of 5%.

Another important factor of the Chinese rural system reform has been the gradual relaxation of the residence registration,[6] *hukou*, which beginning in the early 1990s permitted unemployed workers in their original hukou area to migrate to other areas.[7]

At the industrial level, the reforms promoted by Deng Xiaoping involved the "opening to the outside world" for a period of 100 years. This opening up took place in stages and was referred to by Deng as "The Great Experiment" by attracting foreign investment and the recuperation of coastal areas that, in the nineteenth century, had been important trade areas with the outside world.

Initially, as part of the plan, the Joint Ventures Law was created, permitting foreign companies entry into China, in order to give China's state-owned enterprises access to new technologies and to modernize. To achieve these goals, four strategic regions[8] were created to develop a trading system and to be a place where foreign investments would be welcomed[9] (Zemin 2002). These are the so-called Special Economic Zones (SEZs) which, among other characteristics, have lower tax rates than the rest of the country (Masiero 2006) and count on a vast reserve of local labor and migrants.

Within these regions, special tariff systems were introduced, reducing the administrative procedures for importing and exporting products and, more specifically, a minimum tariff and, at the limit, exemption from duties on inputs intended to be used in the production of goods for the international market.

Therefore, Shenzhen, due to its proximity to Hong Kong, was singled out to become the first SEZ, attracting numerous international companies to the region. In fact, as Cunha & Acioly (2009) point out, the regions where the SEZs were installed were "handpicked" in order to attract the largest amount of investments.

Later on, in 1984, new packages of liberalization were launched, creating 14 more cities open to attract foreign capital, among them is Shanghai. After Deng Xiaoping's trip to southern China in 1993 – he witnessed the prosperity of the region compared to the rest of the country – an additional 18 zones were created. In the 2000s, dozens of investment attraction regions were created, this time in China's interior, in an attempt to bring development to other parts of the country.[10]

Due to the industrial establishment in these regions, and thanks to the relaxation of the hukou system, there was an intense migration process from rural populations to coastal cities seeking industrial jobs. To get an idea of this process, in 1978, the urban population in China consisted of 170 million inhabitants. Today, this number is around 700 million. Part of the migrant[11] contingent is not being absorbed by the industries and they end up returning to rural areas, because in some provinces the Hukou continues to be very strict when it comes to ensuring access to health and education for people coming from other regions. But, the portion of migrants absorbed has been critical to Chinese economy, accounting for 20% of China's GDP growth, according to studies by the Chinese Academy of Social Sciences (Changhong 2004).

The result of this opening process allowed China's GDP to grow at an annual rate of 10% on average. Numerous multinational companies have settled in the country, mainly in the Guangdong region, where there are more than 400,000 factories, representing 35% of China's national exports.

According to data from the United Nations Conference on Trade and Development (Cunha & Acioly 2009), until 1991, the flow of foreign investments into China was less than US$5 billion per year. However, due to the attraction of new international capital resulting from Deng's trip to southern China, this amount increased to US$60 billion by the end of the 1990s, and in 2007, it reached $83 billion, increasing the stock of foreign investment in China to $327 billion.

Chinese reforms in labor relations

If, in the economic aspect, there were profound changes in the post-Mao period, they were also intense in the area of labor relations leading to two major labor laws that I will briefly discuss here. The first one resulted from the privatizations of Chinese state-owned companies that brought millions of workers into China's labor market. The second one was not caused by privatization, but by the process of rural expropriation and the migration of millions of people from the countryside to the Chinese cities.

From a historical point of view, the genesis of this movement was due, firstly, to government's decision, announced at the *National Conference on Work and Employment* in 1980, to reduce unemployment by encouraging people to create self-employment opportunities through small businesses, craft workshops, etc. Furthermore, the government created numerous Labor Service Agencies (*laodong fuwu gongsi*), meant to help the unemployed to get jobs. In practical terms, this meant that the labor issue was slowly moving from the hands of the CCP into the hands of the Chinese workers.

Another element of this process relates to the increased competition suffered by state-owned enterprises from private companies in some regions of China, due to the country's openness to attracting foreign capital.[12] Until the mid-1980s, state-owned companies controlled 75% of China's economy and employed 85% of the urban labor force. However, with the economic opening, the state-owned companies started to compete directly with foreign companies, losing market and money to the latter. In an attempt to change such economic scenario, the government changed the labor relations model of the Chinese manufacturing world, whose main measures were the introduction of bonuses and premiums to increase worker productivity, the labor contract system, and the implementation of productivity-based wage levels.

Perhaps the most significant measure is the labor contract system, because it changed the worker's relationship with the Chinese state. The latter would no longer continue to employ individuals for their entire life. Now, this relationship would be based on a contract that could be undone if the worker did not meet management's objectives, which, despite being associated with the CCP, began to operate under the market economy's molds.

The key point of this change occurred in 1986, when the State Council issued a regulation allowing state-owned enterprises to recruit workers through employment agencies, introduce contract labor for both new and old workers, and dismiss those who did not conform to the new managerial requirements.

From 1986 onward, all state-owned enterprises started to operate under these new terms. The contract became a requirement and extinguished the employment relationship based on *universal lifelong employment*, which increasingly handed workers over to the dictates of corporate management.

Although these reforms left workers with no protection, a complete restructuring of the Chinese labor force occurred in the early 1990s through a national privatization program. During this restructuring program – which coincided with the historical period of privatizations in Latin America and especially in Brazil – the government invited foreign investors to acquire state-owned companies that were performing inefficiently and losing competitiveness in the international market. From the beginning of privatization until 2001, about 85% of state-owned enterprises had been privatized, many of them under suspicion of corruption committed by the CCP, investors, and former managers. In return for their silence about corruption, they were given positions in the restructured companies (Potter & Jianyong 1996).

The reform process resulted in over 50 million workers being laid off (Lee 2009) and available to the labor market. In other words, the social benefits that comprised the range of worker protection in the Mao Zedong period were removed, instead, they introduced the logic of labor as a "commodity".

The *Iron Rice Bowl* era was over. More and more workers sought their jobs through employment agencies, and many others turned to self-employment as their primary means of earning an income.

In fact, the worker's exploitation in the factories, mainly children and disabled people, reflected the Communist Party's policy, under the "harmonious society" perspective, that prescribed intervention in labor relations as a last resort. This was evidenced because there was no law regulating relations[13] between capital and labor, despite a number of resolutions aimed to regulate labor as a "policy" rather than as a "law" or "legislation".

The inexistence of labor law and the flexibility of resolutions had three aspects: First, the CCP issued the resolutions which were political in nature, without an in-depth discussion of the issue, only of an "administrative nature". Second, most resolutions were full of propaganda language and lacked clarity regarding workers' rights, which made them difficult to enforce. Third, it was difficult to distinguish the resolutions from documents previously issued, such as administrative orders, decrees, rules, and notifications; therefore, they had no practical effect on Chinese labor relations (Gallagher 2005).

In fact, the non-formulation of effective labor legislation was part of the government's own strategy for a quick development of the economy, at the expense of the worker. The main priority was a high GDP growth, therefore, implementing resolutions that made work relations more flexible toward the Chinese economic development project. Another element was labor legislation that implied the existence of conflicts between capital and labor, therefore, something typical of capitalist relations of production, which the CCP wanted to hide.

This process of virtual nonexistence of state interference in the regulation and protection of workers' rights led to a series of problems concerning working conditions, working time, and wage payments. A survey conducted in Beijing in 1993 showed that 12% of urban workers hired by private companies worked 10 to 12 hours a day, 5% worked 12 to 14 hours a day, and another 3% worked more than 14 hours a day. Another problem referred to wage arrears and often, arbitrary cancellation of payment by companies (China Labour Bulletin 2010). The situation for China's rural migrant workers – about 30 million at the time – was even worse: almost 90% of them worked more than 12 hours a day and the media described them as "slaves",[14] as if China was living a situation similar to the early English Industrial Revolution, with labor abuses of all kinds.

That had great international repercussions because NGOs for labor rights and human rights groups began to report this chaos of violations to the international media, which eventually aroused in the workers the feeling that they were not being properly treated by their employers. Thus began a period of upheaval in the factory floor that resulted in numerous strikes at the time. For example, from January to May 1993, there were 194 strikes[15] in 17 provinces in China, involving about 30,000 workers.

The main elements of the 1994 Labor Law

China's first true labor legislation (Labor Law) emerged from this social unrest, supported by international pressure with the help of NGOs, and seemed to be a way to "calm tempers" of the Chinese population. Also supported by the All-China Federation of Trade Unions (ACFTU)[16] and under the Chinese Labor Minister's speech that the "*people came first*", the Labor Law was finally enacted in July 1994.

As can be seen in the text issued at the time by the Chinese government,[17] the Labor Law covered a number of issues concerning workers' rights, such as working hours, contracts, overtime, rest and vacations, and firing and hiring, with the intention of "establishing and safeguarding the labor system suitable for the socialist market economy" (Article 1). It was an attempt to implement a labor standard in China in line with the standards set forth by the International Labor Organization (ILO). Working hours, for example, were set at 8 hours a day and 44 hours a week,[18] with a mandatory one day off per week (Article 36). The overtime limit was set at 3 hours per day, not permitted to exceed 36 hours per month (Article 41). If there was overtime, the employer had to pay 150% of contractual wages if it occurred on normal days, 200% on day-off days, and 300% on mandatory holidays.

The Labor Contract was introduced as a mandatory model for all companies; however, they could make an experience contract for a period of up to six months (Article 21). The Labor Law also introduced the Collective Labor Contract, celebrated between labor unions and the companies. In a company with no union established yet, the contract could be concluded between representatives elected by the workers (Article 34). In relation to wages, the Labor Law gave companies autonomy to determine how payments were allocated and it stipulated that they should be based on productivity (Article 47). However, it stipulated that wages could not be lower than the standard of the provinces where the company was located (Article 48), because at that time there was no mandatory minimum wage covering the entire Chinese territory.[19]

There is also a chapter in the Labor Law dealing with protection for both young and women workers[20] (Article 58). As part of the protection, employers were required to provide regular physical examinations to assess these workers' health (Article 65).

The Law stipulated the following for women employees: a) they should not be engaged to work in mines or places that required great physical exertion (Article 59); b) during their menstrual period, employers could not ask them to work in high places, with high or low temperatures, or permeated by cold water (Article 60); c) from the seventh month of pregnancy on, they could not work overtime or the night shifts (Article 61); d) after giving birth, they would be entitled to no less than 90 days of paid maternity leave (Article 62); and e) during the period of breast-feeding their babies less than one-year old, they were not allowed to work overtime or night shifts, and engage in work with Grade III physical labour intensity (Article 63).

In theory, new China's Labor Law introduced most of the labor rights already enacted in other parts of the world. However, it did not include the right to strike. It continued to be prohibited, subject to dismissal if occurred. This seems to show the Communist Party's reluctance for a broader recognition of the antagonism between workers' interests and those who owned the means of production. This can be seen in the very terms used in the Labor Law largely influenced by the old Mao Zedong ideology. For example, the Law used the term work unit (*danwei*), which, as we have seen, refers to the old Mao era labor system, instead of company or factory, and *laborer* instead of *employee*.

However, one could argue that the Labor Law was a first attempt to lay a relatively solid foundation for the development of labor relations suitable for socialism with Chinese characteristics, and a way to balance the precariousness of the market economy and the socialist idea of Mao Zedong's former command (Josephs 1995).

Limitations in the implementation of the 1994 Labor Law

Despite a large array of worker rights and protection enacted by the Labor Law, its enforcement failed to be effective. For example, labor contracts in China's inner cities have not been implemented. Many employers, especially in the private sector, have neglected to sign contracts and continued to employ workers without legal obligations.

Poor enforcement of the Labor Law is based on four issues. First, one must take into account China's huge supply of workers, much higher than demand,[21] which causes a disadvantage to the working class in relation to employers (Ngok 2008). If workers inquired about the nonexistence of contracts, for example, they might lose their jobs, since "there were a lot of people in line".

Second, the provisions of the Labor Law allowed employers to take actions that were not covered by the legislation. For example, it did not stipulate a time limit for employers to sign the employment contract and did not oblige them to pay compensation when the contract ended. In addition, it did not specify employers' obligations when entering into a probationary contract. If the worker was dismissed during the probationary period, the employer was not required to pay severance pay for the remaining days of the contract. As a result, many workers were fired before the probationary contract ended.

Third, Ngok (2008) notes the lack of inspectors to oversee compliance with the Labor Law. In 2001, there were only 40,000 people responsible for about 240 million workers. Nowadays, in Guangdong Province, for example, the ratio of personnel to inspect labor violations is 1 to 20,000 workers, much lower than the target set by the government, which is 1 to 8,000. Meanwhile, in the provincial capital Guangzhou, there are only 130 specialized supervisors to oversee 160,000 companies.

Fourth, the author emphasizes the lack of strict punishments for employers who failed to implement labor contracts. If contracts were not signed, the Law stipulated that employers would be "warned" by the Labor Administrative Department (Article 98). Only when the work imposed on workers caused serious harm and injury would employers become criminally liable (Article 96).

The weak or almost nonexistent participation of the labor unions could be further included in the law enforcement and the fight for workers' rights. Since it was strictly tied to the leaders of the Communist Party and these, in large part, to private companies, ACFTU did shy away from its role of organizing labor to fight for improvements in labor relations.

Migrant workers and a new labor legislation

Amidst all this leniency and lack of law enforcement, rural workers have remained marginalized from labor protections. This happens because there is a culture in China of disregarding farm workers as "laborers". They work in factories, but are considered by government and employers as "peasants". Therefore, the Labor Law did not recognize them as "migrant workers" and no provision in the law referred to these workers. The term "rural" or "migrant" was not in the Law. It was as if they, rural migrants, were fruitful labor force, but since they were "not workers" they were not legally protected by the same rights of "true urban workers".

This nonrecognition of migrant workers was evident in their wages, they were lower than those of urban workers. Because migrant workers were in a difficult position without any government or union response, many migrant workers left the cities and returned to their rural villages, provoking a labor shortage in the Pearl River Delta and other coastal regions in 2003.

Amidst this migrant labor problem and the nonenforcement of the Labor Law, when Hu Jintao and Wen Jiabao[22] came to power, it seemed that a new direction was given to labor policy. Under the slogan "growth with social investment and environmental protection", the new leaders moved the labor agenda to the center of the political discussion, a fact that can be partially explained by the shortage of migrant labor in the coastal regions, where goods for export are generally produced. This reduction in the labor supply in these regions became a cause for concern on the part of investors and local government officials.

In 2003, to reverse this process, the new government introduced the resolution "Notice on Doing a Better Job Concerning the Employment Management and Services for Migrant Worker" by introducing a policy of principles that proposed: a) abolition of discrimination against migrant workers; b) elimination of nonpayment and arrears of wages for these workers; c) resolution of problems associated with free education for migrant children; d) provision of vocational training; e) the better living conditions including the working environment in urban areas; and f) strengthening and improvement of administrative control over urban workers (Gallagher 2005).

Moreover, amid strikes and work accidents involving migrant workers, the State Council in 2006 issued a policy[23] document declaring for the first time that migrant workers were an important element in the Chinese labor force.

The document also pointed out a series of objectives that should be pursued over the years to come, namely: a) creation of a labor market to unify both rural and urban workers through fair competition; b) promotion of a series of policies to protect the rights of migrant workers; c) creation of a system of public services for migrant workers in both rural and urban sectors; d) strictly regulate employers to ensure that workers are paid, and oblige them to pay no less than the national minimum wage; e) implementation of the labor contract system by strongly controlling employers to eliminate child labor; f) inclusion of migrant workers in workmen's compensation insurance and medical insurance for chronic diseases; g) expansion of urban public services for migrant workers; h) protect the right of rural migrants' families to own land through the family responsibility system; and i) development of small towns permitting them to receive industries and hire local labor.

However, the key step taken by the Chinese government occurred in 2007. Earlier that year, local television showed a report that hundreds of children, some as young as 8 years, had been kidnapped and sold for 500 Yuan each to pottery managers in Shanxi and Henan provinces. The television report caused a national scandal that put pressure on government to implement stronger legislation to prevent such an event from occurring again. In response to popular pressure and amid lobbying from unhappy companies, the government, after four deliberative sessions, issued the Employment Contract Act in June 2007, becoming effective in January 2008.

The main elements of the 2008 Labor Contract Law

The *Labor Contract Law* with its 98 articles[24] is considered the most significant change in labor policy since the 1994 Labor Law. The new law confirms innumerous parameters set forth in 1994, however it introduces new articles and fills in gaps that the old law omitted, as we saw earlier. It also introduces the terms employer and employee instead of labor unit (danwei) and laborer.

The major changes in the 2008 law content are as follows: **a**) reduction of the probation contract period from six to three months; **b**) in case of dismissal during the probation period, the worker is entitled to severance pay for the remaining days of the contract (Article 28); **c**) permitting the worker to file a lawsuit directly against the company, which previously could only be done through a labor union (Articles 30, 32, 72, 77, and 79); **d)** the law states clearly that the employer cannot delay or fail to pay wages, under penalty of being penalized by the inspection agencies (Article 30); **e**) the employer cannot force anyone to work overtime (Article 31); **f**) the worker's refusal to perform dangerous work or any other work that puts his or her physical integrity at risk cannot be considered a breach of contract. If the employer dismisses him/her for that reason, the employee is entitled to go to court (Article 32); **g**) if the company decides to dismiss up to 20 workers, and if these workers make up 10% of the total workforce, it must explain with 30 days in advance to the labor union and workers the reasons for the dismissals, after considering their opinions and after submitting its dismissal plan to the labor administrative department. In case layoffs occur, the employer must keep on the job people with long-term contracts, those who have the job as their only source of income, and those who have children or elderly as dependents. If the employer intends to hire new employees in the six months following the layoff, those who were fired must be notified and will have priority to be rehired under the same conditions set in the old contract (Article 41); **h**) The possibility of part-time work, as long as it does not exceed 4 hours a day and 24 hours a week for the same employer. In part-time work, the hourly rate cannot be less than the hourly rate of the 8-hour contract (Article 68); **i**) the employer cannot retain any identity document from the employee, under penalty of paying 2,000 Yuan for each document retained (Articles 9 and 84); **j**) if a company's workers' wages are lower than the minimum wage set by the government, or if overtime has not been paid, the employer must pay both the wage shortfall and the amount of unpaid overtime. If payment is not made within the period prescribed by the Labor Administrative Department, the employer will be ordered to pay extra compensation to the worker at a rate of at least 50% of both the amount of the wage shortfall and the amount of unpaid overtime (Article 85); **k**) the employer must pay compensation amount in double to the employee in case the contract revocation or termination violates any article of the Labor Contract Law (Article 87); **l**) if the employer illegally detains the employee, or exposes the employee to substandard working conditions that may cause harm to his or her health, the employer will be criminally prosecuted by government agencies (Article 88); **m**) if Human Resource companies violate any of the articles of the Labor Contract Law, a minimum fine of 1,000 Yuan per person will be enforced, and the company will have its business license revoked (Article 92).

In contrast to the aforementioned articles, one can say that, compared to the 1994 Labor Law, the 2008 Labor Contract Law incorporates into the legislation's content norms that aim to combat existing problems of working conditions, lack of a labor contract, and low wages, by directing to more effective punitive action those who violate it. The new law also sounds as an attempt to reposition migrant workers into a proper worker status, by assimilating them as part of the national labor force.

However, despite this path pursued by the law, Chinese migrant workers continue to be the major victims of precarious work and the nonobservance of labor rights. Even after the enactment of the new law, the old forms of exploitation of these workers did not cease to exist. Nevertheless, this Chinese group of workers has gained plenty of knowledge concerning the labor laws and has built a greater network of solidarity and communication among themselves using the web. Therefore, they have become more active in fighting for their rights, less fearful of some kind of repression, and seeking the social welfare promised to them by CCP some time ago.

China's management and work processes: at home[25]

In addition to economic reforms and labor legislation, the changes occurred in China are also expressed through different forms of labor force management, indicating that China's manufacturing structure accommodates different labor regimes (Liu 2010). From this point of view, Chinese state-owned companies and private companies, for example, have important qualitative distinctions. But, more than that, productive territories within China itself have different labor process arrangements, and therefore, it is not possible to speak of a single manufacturing pattern.

Following this analytical path, Lüthje, Luo, & Zhang (2013) sought to differentiate labor regimes in China and identified four different "patterns" of labor organization: Chinese state-owned enterprises, joint venture enterprises, export-oriented private companies, and subcontracted companies.

Chinese state-owned enterprises are characterized by relative stability in their production conditions, compliance with national labor laws, and a strong labor union presence. On the other hand, joint ventures tend to copy Western production styles and plant organization, paying high wages and investing in worker qualification and education. In these companies, regulation of employment relationship is made through individual employment contracts, without any collective agreements made with labor unions (Lüthje, Luo, & Zhang 2013).

On the other hand, export-oriented private companies are a mix of high and low levels of employment relationship, showing different labor sub-regimes, with different wage levels, the number of hours and work intensity, and regimes of managerial hostility. As for subcontracted companies, the authors identify factories in the garment, toy, and shoe industries that combine a modern production structure with intense flexibilization of employment and a large scale of exploration of migrant workers, which includes overtime beyond the legal limit, payment of low wages, and inexistence of labor unions.

Lee (2007), on the other hand, divides China's labor processes between "sunrise" and "sunset" industries, each of them having its own management regime and labor supply. The former are export-oriented factories located around the Chinese coast, which can also be referred to as the "Guangdong model". The latter are the old state-owned industries that have been reformed, located in northern China. The author makes this distinction when she analyzes the changes in Chinese state-owned enterprises (SOEs) after privatization in the 1990s and early 2000s. For Lee, SOE privatization created a managerial movement from organized dependence to disorganized despotism.

Under the "organized dependence" system, the state-owned companies offered pensions, medical care, maternity benefits, unemployment insurance, and accident allowances to workers. In addition, management was willing to listen to workers and offered bonuses according to work progress and annual wage increases, becoming an overly "paternalistic factory" or "patron-clientelist".

After privatizations, this structure was broken. The "disorganized despotism" was established, meaning that dependency on migrant labor, through low wages and no workers' benefits; unregulated labor, the creation of net of subcontractors; contract through large-scale production; and authoritarianism in the workplace, as manufacturing processes started to be determined by the managers themselves, with no worker participation (Smith & Liu 2016). In addition, many benefits and bonuses were eliminated and workers from state-owned companies were pressured to resign.

For Lin (2016), this process described by Lee developed into what the author calls "managerial despotism". After analyzing a Chinese state-owned company in the naval area, the author shows the managerial tricks which came into effect after the restructuration undergone by the SOEs. For example, the company began employing workers through collective bargaining contracts or outsourcing production to "workshops". Because these collective agreements and workshop work offer lower wages, factory management has sought to push workers into this arrangement.

Another form of this "despotism" is the creation of a labor organization based on "production quotas" with the promise of wage increases when targets are met. However, according to the author, this agreement has not been fulfilled. That is made even worse because the 2008 Labor Contract Law states that workers' wages must be increased on an annual basis, therefore managers started to lower the bonuses in order to reduce the overall cost of labor.

At the shop-floor level of organization, the author highlights that workers' participation in decisions has been increasingly put on the back burner, because work management started to be based on line leaders and no longer on "section chiefs", who were chosen by the workers themselves and who enjoyed great prestige among the workers.

In this type of factory organization, decisions on work process had to go through these "section chiefs", who offered some factory resistance to managerial tricks. However, the reforms of the state-owned companies eliminated this role, giving the line leader a "managerial status". If before the leader's salary and bonus were organized by HR as "shop floor" salary, with the changes, they started to be listed as managerial sector salaries, seeking to show that, now, leaders were part of the organizational sector from factory.

According to the author, this encouraged line leaders to be in line with the managers' interests and strive to improve production, thus eliminating the possibility of line leaders leading labor resistance (Lin 2016). This process leads the author to conclude that the relative democratic factory of the early state-owned reforms has transformed it into a despotic factory, where managers dictate the rules to workers on the shop floor.

Indicating a tangled form of labor management underway in China, managerial models such as Quality Circles, information sharing, and employee complaint channel are pointed out by Lu (2016) as strategies introduced by a Chinese state-owned company in the metalworking sector to cope with labor union presence and "modernize the factory". The author calls these new tricks a kind of direct participation regime. The old system, organized by labor union, Lu (2016) calls representative participation regime. Coupled with this process, the company's HR, which previously had a merely bureaucratic role (payment of salaries and benefits), now has key importance in implementing the new management methods in an attempt to leverage productivity, efficiency, and create loyalty to the company.

Despite the fact that the majority of workers approve the new managerial methods of participation – which according to Lu (2016), happens because the company still has a "paternalistic" posture by providing education for employees' children, transportation, and shopping facilities, thus creating a control-consent relationship – these management techniques have been rejected by younger managers, who consider them too similar to the prescriptions of the old state-owned enterprises. Instead, they advocate flexibility in employment relations and managerial rigidity, associating this with the success and expansion of Chinese multinationals around the world.

In a different state-owned company in the heavy machinery sector, Jia (2016) points to a type of work which she calls the "Dualistic Labor Regime". This type of work organization has been used as a means for state companies to reduce labor costs by using intensively subcontracted workers, who live together in the same factory space and perform the same functions as the "formal" workers, therefore the factory dualism. But, unlike formal workers, "informal" workers, who have no qualifications and no high school education, are hired by "contractors", work two shifts, and suffer constant threats of being fired. Meanwhile, "formal" workers are not forced to work overtime, or fired for that matter. When there are attempts to do so, they organize and protest.

In order to reduce resistance from what management considers "rebel workers", the company began to organize production through a dual "formal"/"informal" relationship, and by paying a piece-rate wage. When products are in demand, the number of tasks for "formal" workers is reduced. When they produce the same products, the pay for the subcontracted workers is higher, therefore creating an antagonism between these two categories of employees, undermining possible bonds between them and causing, in many cases, "formal" employees to resign and be replaced by the "informal" ones.

As pointed out by Smith & Zheng (2016: 369), while rejecting this idea of "mixing" work arrangements, other authors have seen a form of "bloody Taylorism"[26] prevailing in China. Based mainly on research conducted in Foxconn factories around the country, these studies indicate work processes with characteristics of discipline and military ideologies, simplification of tasks, intensive work (60 hours per week), unpaid overtime, heavy use of migrant labor,[27] forced student labor, a combination of production and reproduction of the workforce in large industrial centers functioning as "closed cities", and payment of low wages. This has led to not only worker suicides but also innumerous strikes, conflicts between workers and the police, and collective resistance (Chan & Pun 2010; Pun & Chan 2012).

Despite these elements, as Smith & Liu (2016: 3) show, we need to be cautious when talking about Chinese companies. On the one hand, Foxconn is a very specific case, which cannot be the "paradigm" for what happens in China, as a whole. On the other hand, Huawei company has introduced long-term labor relations between workers, investments in technological innovations, qualification, and training, as well as co-ownership between workers and companies, for example.

Moreover, the idea of a dominant labor model in China can lead people to ignore the important transformations that have been observed throughout the country, especially in terms of wage values.[28] In recent years, they have been growing at an annual rate of about 10%, above the other developing countries in Asia. This led Guangdong Province in 2016 to announce that it would freeze the local minimum wage for the next two years, in an attempt to prevent businesses from leaving to other Chinese regions or even overseas.

The speech by China's Vice Minister of Human Relations and Social Security, Xin Changxing, in July 2016, also pointed in that direction.[29] According to him, "Our advantage in labor costs is no longer as clear-cut as before. We should ease the frequency and scale of wage increases so as to preserve our competitive advantage".

Seen from a broad perspective, this process indicates that China, after decades of wage and employment transformations, can no longer be considered an abundant and inexhaustible source of cheap labor. And that is evidenced when one compares the country's average minimum wage with other Asian countries in the region, which places China behind South Korea and Japan, but no longer alongside the Philippines and Vietnam. In fact, it is the latter countries that have become the "alternative" to China's rising wages. Graphic 2.1 presents an outline of this process. Another dimension of this process currently underway in China can be observed in Graphic 2.2, which shows the country's position in the Asian economic spectrum, with a focus on average salaries. If, in 2003, they amounted to a little over $100, today China's average salary is over $600, which is higher than the average of

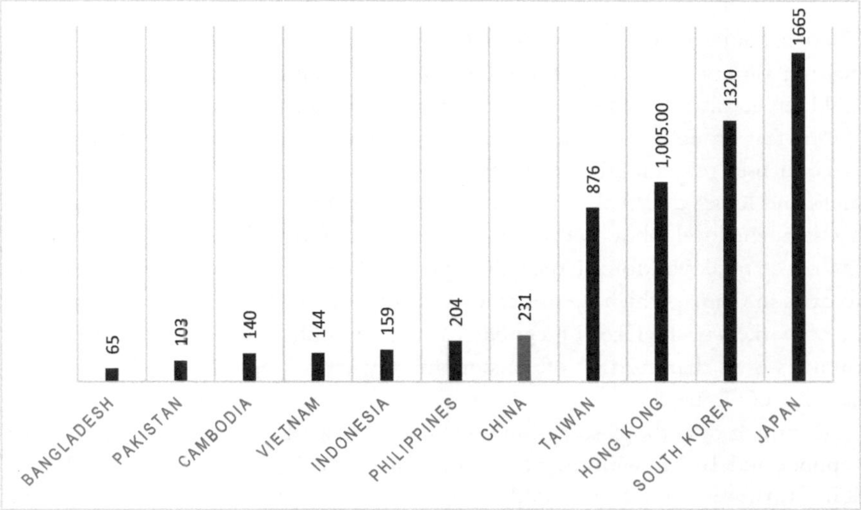

GRAPHIC 2.1 – Average minimum wage in Asia (2016) – (US$)

Source: China Labour Bulletin. Author's adaptation.

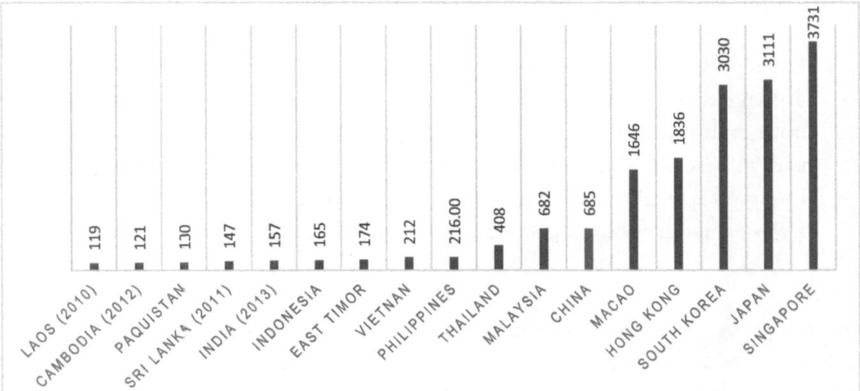

GRAPHIC 2.2 – Average Asian wages (2014–2015) – (US$)

Source: Prepared by the author based on data from ILO and the China Statistical Yearbook.

countries like Thailand and Malaysia, but lower than Macao and the Hong Kong region with salaries around $1,646 and $1,836, respectively, recorded in 2016.

Note that this average wage incorporates the country's economic activity from the urban space only. It compares the wage levels of both the state-owned companies and private companies located in China and relates to 2014–2016, with the exception of countries with an indication of previous years.

China's management and work processes: far from home

When it comes to Chinese companies' behavior outside of China, studies have shown a variety of works permeating Chinese capital in different regions of the world, especially Africa and Europe, particularly Eastern Europe.

One fact brought up by the most recent studies is that in the Czech Republic, Foxconn uses migrant labor from Romania and Bulgaria as a way to pay lower wages and lower their costs, as well as recruits workers via employment agencies that segment local labor. Moreover, temporary workers already represent almost 50% of the total workforce (Andrijasevic & Sacchetto 2016). But unlike Foxconn's factories in China, which do not employ workers above the age of 35, the average age of workers in the Czech Republic has been around 30 to 50 largely due to the country's own characteristic of its economically active population, which is older than that of China.

According to authors, something that connects work at Foxconn in the Czech Republic and Turkey with their plants in China is the high turnover rate. While in China, turnover at Foxconn is in the range of 50% per year, in the Czech Republic this rate is around 30%, and in Turkey, around 25%. This turnover rate is caused by the high level of production fluctuation, high speed of operational tasks, low wages, and repetitive work (Andrijasevic & Sacchetto 2016).

An example of how the type of work is performed in the factory is given by one of the workers interviewed by Andrijasevic & Sacchetto (2016: 342):

> Each person has five tasks to perform on the assembly line. That's all we do: take a computer screen and place it in front of us, take a cable and push both ends into the machine, take the cooler and push it inside and then the part moves on. One repeats this the whole time. When I first came here, I worked an eight-hour shift on the assembly line and it was so repetitive that I was no longer thinking straight but instead worked like a machine.
>
> *(Slovak worker)*

On these production lines, the most important positions – supervisors and foremen – are held by the Chinese. For "local" workers, access to higher positions is only possible for those who have some command of the Czech language, rising to the level of line leader at best. It is also noteworthy the intensive use of female labor, women around 25 years of age. This cutoff by age is part of the manufacturing policy of the Chinese in Europe, which, according to Andrijasevic & Sacchetto (2016: 343) "are prejudiced against women in their 30s or older and consider them too slow to work on assembly jobs".

In terms of wages, the hourly wage for a permanent worker in the Czech Republic is around €3.5, about €600 to €700 per month. When compared to the country's average wage – which in 2012 was about €750 – and the minimum wage of €330, Foxconn workers earn less than the national average wage, but well above the minimum wage. In Turkey, wages for production line workers are just above the minimum wage, which is set by government and revised periodically (Andrijasevic & Sacchetto 2016: 343).

The highest wage difference will be among temporary workers, who are paid 2.5 euros per hour worked, or 400 to 500 euros per month. As a result of the language differences among production line workers, they rarely communicate among themselves, making it difficult for them to stand together and fight for wage improvements. Therefore, this leads to a feeling of isolation, as well as divisions among workers (Andrijasevic & Sacchetto 2016: 343).

This is made more serious because the local authorities – in their attempt to attract Chinese capital – are more involved with the companies' interests than with those of the workers. But, they are not the only ones, the labor unions themselves are also involved. In the case of Turkey, the Turk is[30] well known for pursuing the class "compromise" policy with neoliberal agenda. In the Czech Republic, such kind of "compromise" has practical repercussions on the country's factory floor, as Andrijasevic & Sacchetto (2016: 353) show:

> The role of the union in creating divisions between the domestic and foreign workforces is clearly discernible in Foxconn's plants in the Czech Republic. . . . While certainly applied by management, the vertical division between direct workers and agency workers is reinforced by the trade union's disinterest in migrant workers' conditions. When it comes to migrant agency workers, the trade unions' position is that they should be employed only on a temporary basis and exclusively as an interim unskilled substitute for domestic Czech workers.

Besides those issues, another crucial characteristic of the Chinese presence in Europe is the "factory dormitory" policy. While in Turkey all workers live in apartments or family homes and have to commute more than 30 minutes on buses rented by the Chinese company to reach the factory, in the Czech Republic – as is the case in China – most migrant workers live in dormitories[31] (Andrijasevic & Sacchetto 2016).

The difference between the Czech Republic and China is that dormitories in the Czech Republic are single rooms built out of old army camps or former factories located away from the workplace. In China, dormitories are part of huge complexes that gather in a single space the factory, dormitories, and basic service areas, such as beauty parlors, cafeterias, and lan houses (Smith & Pun 2006). In order to demonstrate the similarity between the two countries, we can use the words of Andrijasevic & Sacchetto (2016: 348) in the sense that "dormitories facilitate the extension of management's control over labour in a way that intertwines the spheres of life and work".

In Italy, as shown by Wu & Liu (2014), many Chinese companies are accused of abuse of workers' rights, violating labor laws, failing to comply with local legislation that regulates the number of hours that can be worked each week, and putting workers' health and safety at risk.

> In Veneto, for instance, Chinese migrant workers were keenly aware of the poor working conditions of Chinese-owned factories, which was also openly acknowledged by entrepreneurs themselves. The differences in working conditions between Chinese- and Italian-owned employment resulted in a strong desire from Chinese migrant workers to work for Italian employers.
>
> *(Wu & Liu 2014: 100)*

In France and Italy, there are reports of forms of labor control by paying low wages in an attempt to inhibit the mobility of Chinese workers who migrated to these countries, in addition to labor trafficking:

> A legal cover is usually used. The simplest way is to create a limited company in the form of a small enterprise, which conceals 'underground' workshops and makes invoicing possible. The managers or owners of the company (generally two or three people) are the only persons declared legally. Clandestine workers are completely hidden in the workshops. Another method is to declare the legal workers in the workshop but not to declare a further group of clandestine workers who work at night. Subcontracted operations are the most difficult to monitor; the company transfers production tasks to subcontractors who are usually small in size (often producing at home) and widely dispersed. This kind of domestic production is easily concealed, as the locations are inconspicuous and residential. Moreover, owners of such companies do not have to meet social, tax and hygiene obligations.
>
> *(Gao 2004: 9)*

Research studies by Burgoon & Raess (2014) have shown how worried European unions have been about the Chinese presence, accusing the factories of being unresponsive to labor demands. Coupled to this, many Chinese companies have been accused of paying wages below the local subsistence level and of using slave labor in production processes.

Several authors also argue that the Chinese investment in Europe may resemble a "Trojan Horse", undermining policies and laws aimed to protect human rights and labor rights in the region. According to this widespread view on the European continent, many see China as an authoritarian investor that, with its "Dominating Government", could destroy Western capitalism and the old continent's welfare state.

According to Meunier (2012), the arrival of Chinese capital is a combination of opportunity and challenge for Europe. She advocates a strategic coordination of the region's leaderships, because the risks of receiving Chinese capital are smaller than the benefits they provide, among them are the following: a greater flow of capital to countries with financial difficulties, the opening of the European Union to foreign capital, and investment from China directed to the continent and not to hostile or competing countries.

Some researchers on the African continent have addressed concerns that the arrival of Chinese capital would turn the region into a sinosphera. Others question whether China is promoting a new colonization process on the continent (Hung 2018; Bodomo 2019).

With extensive ethnographic research and studies in both Zambia and Tanzania, Lee's (2009; 2017) research provides a different perspective by showing that Chinese capital has more relation complexity than global capital due to its diversity of capitals, thereby, labor diversity and political ties between China and the countries where its companies move into. According to the author, the result is that global capital seeks profit maximization, while Chinese capital has a wide range of objectives.

China's strategic state-owned companies, such as copper mining, have a broader agenda than financial profit, because they also seek "political profit", diplomatic and geostrategic profit, something Lee calls *profit optimization*. Therefore, they would be more flexible and negotiable with politically organized society and national states than traditional global capital, as was the case in Zambia's copper mines; while Chinese companies in the cyclical products market would provide more flexible and precarious jobs, as in Tanzania's textile industries.

From that categorization, Lee's perspective questions and relativizes the possible generalized Chinese predation or colonization of the African continent by positioning specific contexts and agents in those regions and focusing on the idea that China has a range of capital, therefore a variety of accumulation: both by profit maximization and by profit optimization.

Summary

This set of international research indicates a broad range of approaches on Chinese companies both at home and abroad. For South America, as a whole, studies have focused on the type of capital, expansion strategies, and earning possibilities for the local countries when analyzing Chinese investments, including the impacts on local industrialization. Also China's plans in considering the political changes on the continent is shown in studies by Burlamaqui (2015), Cintra & Pinto (2017), Nascimento & Maynetto (2019), Escher & Wilkinson (2019), and Saraiva & Silva (2019).

In line with these international researches around the planet and trying to understand Chinese capital through an empirical study in Brazil, I wanted to know how it behaves in a major region of the world today – the Amazon – which has an economic zone with a variety of industries and markets, where part of the global capital is a reference for production, management, and labor benefits, including a civil society which is historically organized and combative. Moreover, in a context where Chinese capital is started to be seen as an invader and predator of good work practices in the region.

The central argument to be addressed will be that, under ZFM context, connections between headquarters and Chinese subsidiaries are stronger and more coordinated than those of global capital, because they use a state/planning culture to gain some advantages, even though it restricts the creation of strong ties with the territories where they settle. It is part of what I call the *Chinese Production Model*, which begins to be discussed in the following chapter.

Notes

1 The Chinese Nationalist Party (Kuomintang) controlled China's government from 1928 to 1949. Today, its influence is limited to Taiwan, where it is a majority.
2 The work units were a space where employees from certain companies lived. They were located in urban centers next to the workplace.
3 In 1996, the period was extended to 30 years.
4 The one-child policy was enacted in the late 1970s to curb the country's population growth, by restricting many families to a single child. There were some exceptions, for example, couple who lived in the rural areas could have two children; families were allowed to apply to have a second child if their first born was male. In 2013, there was some loosening, allowing urban couples to have the second child, but only if one parent was an only child. The law ended in 2015.
5 As a comparison, Brazil has about 400 million potential arable lands.
6 O *hukou* is a system of household registration used in China since 1950, where every family must have its own registration.
7 Every year, about six million people leave their original area of residence and migrate to other provinces, mainly to those with a large industrial profile, such as Xinjiang, Fujian, Yunan, and Guangdong.
8 Shenzhen, Zhuhai, and Shantou, in Guangdong; and Xiamen, in Fujian Province.
9 The Chinese businesspersons who made most of these investments were from Hong Kong, Macau, and Taiwan, who moved to these regions in the 1950s.
10 Today, China has more than 250 SEZs.
11 Estimates are that by 2020 more than 300 million people will migrate to China's cities.
12 In the early 1980s, four coastal cities were designated as Special Economic Zones in an attempt to attract foreign investment: Shenzhen, Zhuhai, Shantou, and Xiamen. In 1984, this opening-up policy was extended to another 14 coastal cities. The "Opening to the World", conceived by Deng Xiaoping in 1979, was being implemented.
13 Between 1979 and 1994, more than 160 labor resolutions were issued, but they were "principles" and not really "laws". That is, they were a sort of guide for labor relations, rather than something that had to be enforced. Therefore, "noncompliance" with the resolutions did not impose penalties on the companies.
14 On November 19, 1993, a fire broke out at the Zhili toy factory in Longgang Province, Shenzhen District. Because the factory had no emergency exits, the fire killed 84 people and injured 40 more. The incident was widely reported in the international media. Most of the victims were migrant workers from rural areas of China.
15 Workers are not allowed to strike because the government considers it a crime.
16 Founded on May 1, 1925, the National Federation of Trade Unions of China is the largest trade union organization in the world with 169 million members.
17 Ver: www.ilo.org/dyn/natlex/docs/WEBTEXT/37357/64926/E94CHN01.htm.
18 In March 1995, the Chinese State Council reduced the number of working hours to 40 hours a week.
19 The minimum wage system as a national standard was introduced in 2004. Before that, the provinces were responsible for determining the minimum wage level for their localities.
20 The working age limit was fixed at 16 years of age and above. Up to 18 years of age, the law considered it juvenile work.
21 Most of the oversupply of workers was related to rural workers migrating to the industrial cities. By 2005, the number of migrants had reached 130 million people. However, from 2007 on, the demand–supply balance began to stabilize.

22 Installed in 2003 as president and prime minister, respectively. They held these positions until March 2013.
23 The State Council. The Notice on Doing a Better Job Concerning the Employment Management of and Services for Migrant Workers. Beijing, 2003.
24 Ver: http://en.cnci.gov.cn/Law/LawDetails.aspx?ID=6079&p=1.
25 This section is mainly based on the debate made by Smith & Zheng (2016).
26 Alain Lipietz's terminology.
27 Foxconn's total workforce in China comprises migrant workers, more than 85%.
28 Nevertheless, it is important to stress that the growth in salaries is more evident in the big cities. In the interior of the country, for example, there are regions where the minimum wage is below U$S150.
29 www.reuters.com/article/us-china-employment-wages-idINKCN0ZO091.
30 Turkey Metal Workers Union.
31 In China, factory dormitories function as a means of controlling not only the worker's work but also their lives and mobility, closing off possibilities of access to other factories, among others. Smith (2003) refers to this type of control as the "Dormitory Labor System". For more details, see also Smith & Pun (2006).

3

A TROPICAL SILK ROAD

Capital and genesis of Chinese production model in the Amazon

Chinese expansion toward the southern hemisphere

Starting in the late 1990s, China has been seeking foreign markets to expand its capital and increase the country's geopolitical participation in the new world order. Not surprisingly, under the government's strategic direction, Chinese globalization has pursued an upward and high-speed path during this millennium, by expanding its investments for 13 straight years in more than 150 countries with an annual average expansion of 33.6% (Cariello 2021).

This process became prominent in 2008–2009, when the Western powers went through a strong economic crisis and China established itself as one of the protagonists on the world stage, internationalizing its companies and competing with Western capital. Then, in 2013, the Chinese strategy became even clearer with the creation of the project called the Belt and Road Initiative (BRI) or the "New Silk Road". Under Beijing's leadership and with the participation intention of more than 140 countries, this project aims to create a distinctive global flow of capital, services, and communication centered on the Chinese economic structure and political influence.

During this succession of rapid growth and search for projecting international power, as early as 2016, China had a historic record of nonfinancial investments abroad, amounting to $170.11 billion and projects associated with 7,961 companies located in 164 countries and regions (Cariello 2021). This was the first time that the country's total investments abroad exceeded the amount received domestically.

The Chinese external race is related to what Premier Zhu Rongji referred to in 2001 as the "going outside" strategy designed to achieve the following objectives: a) gain access to raw materials (oil, iron, steel, and wood) necessary for a continuous economic growth; b) guarantee food supply needed by a population that has already surpassed 1 billion four hundred million individuals; c) enter other

DOI: 10.4324/9781003229377-3

countries' consumer markets via joint ventures or by purchasing other companies; d) set up plants in their industrial parks; e) influence geopolitical regions traditionally shadowed by Western powers; f) export surplus capacity from Chinese companies; and g) make profits.

Having these objectives in mind, Brazil has emerged as a key partner in helping to achieve Chinese capital's interests in South America, especially after the collapse of Brazilian contractors involved in the corruption scandal known as "Lava Jato" (Car Wash).

However, recent history shows that the two countries have not always been close. After the Chinese Communist Revolution, Brazil distanced itself from China, maintaining diplomatic relations with Taiwan only. Nevertheless, in 1974, the Brazilian military government recognized the People's Republic of China as the Chinese people's representative and broke ties with Taiwan. As a result of this rapprochement, the Brazilian Military President, João Batista Figueiredo, visited China in 1984, followed by President José Sarney, by the end of the dictatorship in Brazil. The restoration of diplomatic relationship has unfolded into numerous technological and scientific partnerships, most notably the joint satellite program for monitoring earth and climate resources (CBERS).

A major breakthrough in the Chinese–Brazilian dialogue took place in 1993, with the visit of Vice-Premier Zhu Rongji – who also visited the PIM – and President Jiang Zemin to Brazil. Called the Sino-Brazilian Strategic Partnership, this bilateral agreement was based on the common objectives of both countries to join efforts to penetrate the gates of the international political-economic agenda. On the other hand, it was primarily anchored on Chinese interest to gain access to agricultural products and raw materials in a rapidly expanding China.

On the Brazilian side, the interest was to preserve and enhance bilateral space cooperation and to use China's infrastructure deficiencies as a springboard for Brazilian service exports to that country (Leão 2011).

In a second phase, which lasted until 1999, Brazil's main objective aimed, above all, the *Energy Cooperation Project*, an attempt to secure important construction contracts for Brazilian contractors in China's dam sector. The latter, in turn, was more interested in increasing iron ore supplies from *Companhia de Mineração Vale do Rio Doce* than in acquiring Brazilian services in hydroelectric plant construction. Similarly, it focused its attention on Brazil's potential to supply food to China, mainly soybeans (Biato Junior 2010).

The third phase of the Strategic Partnership starts in the early 2000s, marked by China's entry into the World Trade Organization, to the present day. Over that period, Brazilian exports to China grew by more than 500%, displacing Japan as its main trading partner and priority destination in the Asian region. If, in 2000, Brazilian exports to China totaled US$1 billion, in 2014, this amount rose to US$40 billion and, in 2021, almost US$70 billion.

This figure placed China as Brazil's main export destination, absorbing more than one-third of Brazil's total exports. The Joint Action Plan 2010–2014 and the Ten-Year Plan 2012–2021 were signed in 2010 and 2012, respectively, and the volume of Chinese capital already invested in Brazil and the ones announced indicate the two countries' interest in maintaining the path of cooperation.

During this stage of the partnership, the Chinese capital flow in Brazil has shown accelerated growth. For example, data indicate that between 2007 and 2020, Chinese companies carried out 176 ventures in Brazil, and investments totaling US$66.1 billion putting Brazil as the recipient of almost 50% of Chinese investments in South America (Cariello 2021).

It is worth noting that 48% of investments confirmed between 2007 and 2020 were directed toward the electric power sector – with a strong presence of the giants State Grid and China Three Gorges. Other investments were in gas and oil extraction in the Brazilian coast (28%), metallic minerals extraction (7%), manufacturing industry (6%), infrastructure works (5%), agriculture, livestock, and related services (3%), and financial services activities (2%).

With a strong presence of government capital – more than 16 SOEs are installed in Brazil – the new Chinese enterprises have created more than 30,000 jobs in the country and kept about 140,000 jobs with the acquisition of existing projects. Moreover, they have been directed to several different Brazilian regions, showing not only diversification of capital but also particular Chinese interests wherever they install themselves. For example, along the coast of the country, we find the central state-owned companies involved in energy. In the mid-west – an agribusiness zone – the prominent role of Chinese capital is in the production, processing, and exportation of agricultural products. In the northeast, the Chinese have a stake in wind and solar energy projects, fiber optic networks, and road and railroad construction.

In the case of the Amazon, two Chinese interests show that China is attempting to implement part of its Belt and Road Initiative in one of the most coveted regions of the world.

The first front concerns Chinese advances in infrastructure, food, and raw material projects. In this process, we can point out: the creation of the "Tapajós River Logistics Corridor" which establishes a grain route between Brazil and China with lower operating costs; it envisions construction of rail lines, roads, and port structures, a project connecting the city of Manaus with Suriname (where almost 10% of the population is of Chinese origin), the search for ores in the Amazon, especially gold, tin, aluminum, iron, copper, and manganese, many of them located on indigenous lands or in environmental preservation areas; the construction of hydroelectric plants and dams, under the leadership of the Chinese state giant China Three Gorges; and land acquisition by Chinese companies.[1]

Another Chinese advance focuses on the manufacturing sector, serving SOEs – those that produce durable consumer goods – and private companies. These enterprises aim to achieve two of China's objectives: to put its state-owned enterprises in competition with the traditional electro-electronic industries, for example, and open up production and market space for a capitalist class willing to participate in the Chinese expansion boom.

This is the reason for the current race to capture part of Brazil's domestic market sales and to export to neighboring countries. There is also intention to control the export of inputs largely used by the Brazilian industry, as I will detail later, something fundamental for the global manufacturing market.

The Amazon emerges in this context as an important space because it has a Free Trade Zone in the city of Manaus – with its distinctive tax system – and an Industrial Park where most of the companies that produce motorcycles, televisions, notebooks, smartphones, air-conditioning, and watches, among other items, in Brazil are based. Manaus also has a specialized labor force with decades of experience in manufacturing these products, at a lower cost than in other Brazilian regions. Furthermore, China wants to enter a market dominated by its Western competitors, such as Europe and the United States, and its Asian neighbors, notably Japan and South Korea.

Chinese presence in the Manaus Free Trade Zone

The Chinese presence in the Manaus Free Trade Zone Industrial Park precedes the arrival of the factories themselves, which are described through two specific phases.

The first one relates to the role played by China, since the 1990s, in the functioning of the Manaus Free Trade Zone exporting input to factories installed in the Amazon. In the new globalization wave and changes in the international division of labor, in general, these factories began to use the Asian country as a source of inputs with high-scale production, low cost, and "continuous addition of technology in production processes" (Pires 2009: 102) (original text in Portuguese). Something was driven by the fact that China fosters manufacturing parks that produce inputs for the global market, especially along the country's coastal region.

In this external scenario, the Industrial Park of the Manaus Free Trade Zone – responsible for more than 90% of the state of Amazonas' imports – was strongly influenced by Chinese production and increased significantly the total amount of inputs imported from China in the 1990s, and at the beginning of the millennium. In 1997, China had an 11% share of the state of Amazonas imports, led at the time by the United States, and followed by Japan and South Korea. However, in the early 2000s, Chinese exports to the state began to increase rapidly and, by 2004, they assumed the first position, representing more than 28% of total imports. In 2015, this amount reached more than 47%, placing Amazonas as a Brazilian state with the highest average imports from China.[2]

The second phase refers to the arrival process of Chinese investments in the Manaus Industrial Park. In a type of economic model, dependent on external investments, such as the Manaus Free Trade Zone, the attraction of Chinese capital has been madeken by public agencies and business associations of Amazonas, using for this specific structures and personnel to manage the state's international relations. In this perspective, the state authorities began to attend economic fairs in China sending missions to the Asian country in an attempt to "advertise" the local potentials.

This is exemplified by participation in the electronic trade fairs in Guangdong and Hong Kong and the reception of Chinese missions arriving in Manaus to prospect the local potentialities. According to the then-secretary of planning for the state of Amazonas, these governmental and corporate actions have been fundamental because, according to him, "the Amazon is, for the Chinese, a new exploration frontier. And once they identify these opportunities, they actually come and settle in" (Interviewed by the author in 2014).

In this search for foreign investments and in light of the Chinese expansion to different parts of the world, it can be observed that China's participation in the PIM has been steadily increasing since the 1990s when compared to the 2000s. For example, although Japan and the United States have dominated investments for several decades, China, between 2008 and 2014, went from just over 2% to almost 10% participation, surpassing countries such as Germany, France, Finland, and Canada. This has happened through acquisition of companies formerly owned by these countries, such as the purchase of IBM, Motorola, and CCE by Lenovo, the Philips (video sector) acquisition by TPV Technology and the joint venture between China's Midea and the American Carrier, which together started manufacturing the Toshiba and Springer brands, only to mention the most recent examples.

This set of Chinese investments in Manaus comprised a total of 22 factories installed until 2017, 13 of them in the electronics subsector (televisions, notebooks, and smartphones), 3 in the mechanical subsector (air conditioners, watches, and home appliances), 2 in the thermoplastic subsector (packaging, vehicle parts, and tape), and 4 in the two-wheeler subsector (motorcycles and bicycles), showing dissemination of investments across various subsectors of PIM. In terms of labor force, those 22 Chinese companies employed about 10,000 workers that year, representing almost 10% of the total labor force in the PIM.[3]

A specter haunts the Amazon: Chinese capital in the local social view

Even before its effects on the economy and labor, one of the first aspects that drew my attention in the field research in the Amazon was the reports from business leaders, unions, and public managers concerning the arrival of Chinese capital. Using a classic expression by Karl Marx, this landing of investments resembled a "specter" circling the region, creating different opinions on the rise and expansion of China around the world and, specifically, its performance in Manaus; it also showed a lack of knowledge about this Asian country and its factories, as we will see.

Some interviewees pointed out that the "success" of China's development occurs because the country is a "capitalist dictatorship" which, according to them, allows it to make economic transformations without internal barriers. Among them are issues involving the environment, labor, and bureaucratic paperwork. Along these lines, so spoke an economist from the Amazonas State Government:

> I see China's advantage in the current global capitalist scenario because it is a dictatorship. It is succeeding in taking advantage of the situation and getting

> into whatever markets it wants to. It is a capitalist dictatorship. And, that is an asset for them, because they are able to act faster, more smoothly.
>
> *(Interview with the author, 2014)*

Similar diagnosis was given by a board of the Federation of Industries of the State of Amazonas (FIEAM), stating that

> the Chinese realized that they were creating millions and billions of hungry people. Then, they realized that they had to pull the people out of starvation. Therefore, they did something that has every chance of working anywhere in the world: Capitalism coupled with dictatorship. If there is a mountain in the way of building a road, they go there and remove the mountain. There is no environmentalist or police, nothing to stop it.
>
> *(Interview with the author, 2014)*

For the interviewee, the Chinese differential would be their ability to carry out the projects without being challenged, something that would not happen in the Amazon due to "radical environmental movement that produces nothing" which, according to him, has been hindering the process of building roads, ports, and waterways connecting the Manaus Free Trade Zone to the rest of Brazil.

In regard to the view held about Chinese factories, the interviewees emphasized, on the one hand, the idea that they would not be creating effective industrial processes in the Amazon, but only assembling *Made in China* products in Manaus. However, they emphasized that the factories must comply with the labor legislation in Brazil.

The president of the Center of Industries of the State of Amazonas (CIEAM) follows this line when he points out,

> China is looking for a market all over the world. They will invest their capital abroad. In the long run, they may become big investors. We have no aversion to the Chinese; they are free to invest. But, here in this city they still do not have a real industrial process. The Chinese companies have no interest in doing this because they bring everything from abroad. They will not do it unless required by law.
>
> *(Interview with the author, 2015)*

Similar reports were also given by public managers of Manaus Free Trade Zone, for whom the "Chinese need to adapt to the local business norms and fit into the labor laws". The first aspect was also highlighted by an FIEAM economist, who stated that the Chinese

> arrive here with the following proposal: "We will install ourselves here in the PIM, but we will bring everything from China." Then the negotiation does not happen. Because there is more than just assembly here. This assembly business in the Free Trade Zone does not exist.[4] Therefore, they must have

> a manufacturing industry. One example is a Japanese motorcycle company, which makes nearly everything here, only 1% is imported.
>
> *(Interview with the author, 2015)*

The leaders of the Metalworkers Union of the State of Amazonas, which represents the workers of the companies surveyed, expressed different views about the presence of Chinese factories in the Manaus Free Trade Zone. For example, the president of the union presented his view in the following terms:

> Among the Asian businessmen, the Chinese are the worst. They bully, they yell at people. There is a very big cultural shock. When they do not adapt to our culture, they are sent back to China. They have this very serious problem. For example, they think that a manager, when he goes to the production line to instruct, has to yell at everybody. They have no respect for collective bargaining agreements, none of them: they do not respect the Brazilian law, which says that you have to work 8 hours and they work 12. . . . Their logic is the following: "if the government fines, how long will it take to solve the problem?" They would rather pay the fine than follow the law, because the damage is less. Therefore, they follow this logic. This type of thing happens in all factories. The social part is even worse: because they have a vision that the important thing is production, they do not care about daycare, they do not care about health care, they don't care about good nutrition. They do not give a damn.
>
> *(Interview with the author, 2014)*

The labor union president also told me about the difficulty that union leaders found in getting Chinese companies to comply with local labor standards, labor norms, and agreements made during class conventions, something that, according to him, was becoming more evident after the 2008 global crisis, which also affected the Manaus Free Trade Zone:

> In general, they do not own their facilities; everything is rented, due to imposition from their country. In fact, these companies are state-owned, not like in Brazil. They come here, but everything is state owned and it is a strategic thing. They do not want to do build anything here. It is different from the Koreans. The Koreans and the Japanese build their own facilities; they know they are going to stay here. Nobody knows about the Chinese. During the 2008 crisis, the factories fired most of their employees. They had created 5,000 jobs, reduced to just 1,000. Therefore, you have these behavioral problems of these Chinese. . . . Another thing: whatever is decided during the workers' agreement, and collective agreement, still have to go to China to receive an approval order. Therefore, because they bring their culture with them, it is complicated for us to make them comply with Brazilian law. We

> have to go to a confrontation. That is why we are going to stop these companies in this first semester.
>
> *(Interview with the author, 2014)*

In addition, the union leader pointed out that the Chinese did not give autonomy to the Brazilian workers and, through the presence of managers, rigidly controlled the production process.

> Production managers are all Chinese. They do not have a Brazilian manager. It is a form of control. Moreover, this is precisely to avoid giving social benefits to Brazilian workers. We, from the union, would rather have them leave Brazil. We do not want this kind of company here, not really.
>
> *(Interview with the author, 2014)*

A union leader who, during the field research, was working in a Chinese company related similar opinion. According to her, the Chinese

> finished with all the good things we had. We worked sitting down; now we all have to stand up. Overtime . . . before we had the right to say no; now we have to work overtime. Therefore, I know that the treatment, the moral harassment is constant there with the workers. They come and want to do as in their country, wanting to hit and yell.
>
> *(Interview with the author, 2014)*

Nevertheless, in the opinion of another union leader, the arrival of the Chinese companies was a new issue and the union was monitoring to see how they would behave in terms of labor legislation, but according to the union president, nothing had happened to justify stopping the factory, at that moment.

Another leader reported that when the Chinese companies arrived in Manaus, noncompliance with labor agreements was constant, and that many of them preferred to pay a fine rather than comply with a determination of the Labor Court. However, according to him,

> This situation has been changing, although very slowly. Look, to have an idea, there was a recent strike there because of bread. They used to give each worker one loaf of bread. Then, the workers started bringing it from home. We went there in the morning and they lifted a bag of bread, which was a way to show us: "look here, we are bringing our own bread because the bosses only give us one". Unless there is pressure from the union, they will not solve it. It is cultural. People there are used to a different culture: once the salary is paid, it is over. There are no more benefits. Therefore, anything that goes beyond the salary they refuse to comply with.
>
> *(Interview with the author, 2015)*

It was within the context of these views concerning Chinese capital's behavior on Amazonian soil that I conducted field research in four Chinese factories installed in the PIM. Despite the preliminary reports pointing to a path, the field data showed a broader and more diverse scenario than that of the "ghost circling the region". The characteristics of the factories, the relationship with the workers of Manaus, and their reaction to the Chinese management will be shown from this point on.

The profile of the surveyed factories

The first company surveyed was MotorChina, a state-owned company belonging to the *China South Industries Group (CSIG)*, one of the world's largest motorcycle manufacturers with 40% of motorcycle production within the Chinese market. It is one of the largest multinationals in the world, employing some 260,000 people, including 40,000 engineers. Founded in 1999, the group is state-owned in China and is divided into several companies that have focused on the photoelectricity, steel, medical, energy, petroleum machinery, firefighting equipment, automobile, and motorcycle markets.

In terms of motorcycle production, the group controls four different brands, among them is MotorChina. For CSIG, the reason for the group's investment focus on the two-wheeler sector in Brazil is because

> CSIG considers Brazil a strategic country. The first in the world to receive the group's largest volume of investments and the first and most important in Latin America. Its main goal is to meet the domestic market with high quality products, affordable prices, and large inventory of spare parts to make the Brazilian consumer aware of how strong one of the world's largest motorcycle manufacturers is.
>
> *(Company information leaflet)*

According to the Manaus plant's industrial director, the decision to move to the Amazon was due to "the tax incentives, different from the other capitals of the country" (Interview with the author, 2014). In 2006, the group installed its headquarters in the city of Fortaleza, in the Brazilian northeast and, in 2008, it arrived in Manaus, where, since then, it has produced five models of motorcycles, all of them aimed at the Brazilian "middle class":

> Our market is the middle and lower middle class. We are aiming at the upper class, with our more robust motorcycle. Nevertheless, the sector has been in decline since 2013. Lower financing and the worsening of the economic scenario caused sales to fall. . . . Our largest market is located in the Brazilian northeast, because we designed our motorcycles for the countryside, for rural areas. However, we want to reach the cities as well.
>
> *(Interview with the author, 2014)*

The Manaus plant, located in the company's owned building, operated on a single work shift, during business hours. The company had about 120 employees, who produced an average of 150 motorcycles a day, with a capacity to produce 30,000 motorcycles a year. Of these workers, 90% were male and 10% female. According to the production management, the prominence of male workers is because the parts used to assemble the motorcycles are heavy and the work is mostly standing: "On the factory floor women are placed where things can't go wrong. Places with many details where only women can perform well" (Interview with the author, 2014).

It is important to note that the company's organizational structure was made up of Chinese nationals. There were about ten expatriates responsible for the company's board of directors, management, and workers' supervision.

The second company researched is called China Board. It is a private company specialized in manufacturing Printed Circuit Boards (PCB). In Manaus, it produces boards for televisions, notebooks, and monitors. It supplies inputs to other factories in the PIM. At the time of the research, it had three customers: one American and two Chinese companies. The company arrived in PIM in the early 2000s and settled in a rented building. Later, a fire broke out in the factory and the entire structure moved to a company's own building, where it is currently installed.

China Board employed about 400 workers – 20 Chinese – divided into two shifts, day shift and night shift, operating production lines with the capacity to produce an average of 10 million boards per year. The company's entire production was sold at PIM, but, according to management, there was production potential to meet national demand. According to one manager, the fact that the production is not exported is a result of the "Brazil cost", which "prevents us from being competitive at the international level" (Interview with the author, 2014).

The third company was ArconChina. Its headquarters is in Zhuhai, a Chinese city in Guangdong Province. It is a state-owned company founded in 1991 and about 49% of the company is under Chinese government control. It is now one of the largest air-conditioning manufacturers in the world, with factories in China, Pakistan, Vietnam, and Brazil. Of all ArconChina's factories, the Chinese plant employs the largest number of workers, according to the company's import manager in Manaus, "Everything at the headquarters is huge. You cannot compare. It is much bigger than the one in Brazil. They have 80 thousand people in the same factory there. Others have, on average, 40 thousand people" (Interview with the author, 2015).

ArconChina arrived in Brazil in 1998, installing its office in São Paulo to analyze the potential of the Brazilian market and determine the best place for installing its factory. Due to the tax incentives offered in Manaus for the air-conditioning sector, ArconChina settled in Manaus in 2001 in a rented building, with investments of around US$ 43 million.

ArconChina was the first Chinese multinational to establish itself in the Manaus Free Trade Zone. In fact, it is also the first subsidiary to be set up outside the Chinese territory. In Manaus, the company operates in one shift (commercial) and states that it does not outsource any part of the production. It produced about 2,000 air conditioners per day and had about 300 employees, 30 of them Chinese, occupying mainly management, engineering, and supervisory positions.

The company had its production aimed at the Brazilian domestic market, but also exported a small part to other countries in South and Central America. Of the companies surveyed, it was the only one with part of its production aimed at exports. All the other companies focused only on the domestic Brazilian market.

The company's import manager, who was Chinese, told me that the major difficulties faced during the process of installation in the Manaus Free Trade Zone were the logistics, the tax and labor legislation, "which is very different from China. But, we hired a consulting company and a lawyer to settle things. Now, everything has been settled" (Interview with the author, 2015).

The fourth company investigated was TVChina, a privately held company, and the largest manufacturer of LCD monitors and screens in the world. It is the fourth largest producer of TVs in the world and one of the 25 largest companies in China, with approximately 25,000 employees in that country alone. This company also has branches in Mexico, Argentina, and Poland.[5]

In 1997, the company arrived in Brazil, opening an office in São Paulo. In 2004, it installed itself in the Manaus Free Trade Zone, in a rented building, manufacturing its own brand of computer and TV monitors, as well as producing for other brands on an outsourcing basis.

In 2008, the company opened another factory in the state of São Paulo, and started to manufacture All-in-One computers and tablets. In 2009, it acquired a license to sell products from a Dutch TV brand. This relationship advanced in 2012, when a joint venture was formed between the companies,[6] and TVChina started manufacturing this European brand's TVs. The company's HR manager explained to me how this process came about:

> The Dutch company's strategy was to focus on a segment where its contribution margin and profits were much higher, the medical equipment sector. The medical division of the Dutch company assembles equipment to equip a complete hospital, from the smallest to the most sophisticated equipment that one can imagine, with 3D technology and everything else. So, it decided to focus on this, because it envisions worldwide view that this is where it has a greater chance of becoming a leader, of making more money and so on. Therefore, seeing that the pressures coming the area of televisions – which became a commodity market with a lot of pressure as far as profits are concerned, and ever more difficult to compete, not only globally but also in Brazil, where it was the leader for a long time. Therefore, it decided that it was not worth it and it would be better to have a partner with a greater competence in the industrial area, which is the case of TVChina.
>
> *(Interview with the author, 2017)*

For the quality manager of TVChina – who was also a manager in the Dutch company – the association between Holland and China was beneficial for both companies, because TVChina could absorb the Dutch know-how in technology. On the other hand, TVChina's know-how in cost reduction was good for the Dutch company.

Meanwhile, the entire monitor production was transferred to São Paulo. But, Manaus continued to produce Chinese brand TVs, Dutch brand TVs, and TVs for other companies, such as Sharp, Panasonic, and Sony. However, in 2014, TVChina bought the Dutch group's share of the joint venture, and became the sole owner of the brand, facilities, and marketing of the Dutch factory, until that point. From then on, the Chinese factory began to develop the industrial technology as well as the production process and marketing.

The company strategically targeted its product toward the upper middle class – a market dominated by Japan's Sony and South Korea's Samsung – using the well-known Dutch brand in order to gain acceptance by consumers.[7] The product with the "proper" Chinese brand focused on the middle class.

In mid-2016, TVChina's monitor production left São Paulo and returned to Manaus. According to the company's management, this change occurred because

> A restructuring for better course and market strategy. With the economic crisis that we are experiencing in Brazil, both TV and monitor sales have dropped considerably. Since the TV market is larger than that of monitors, the most convenient solution would be to unify the two plants in Manaus, since tax incentives for TVs are more significant in Manaus than those for monitors in São Paulo. Through this change, we increased our production in Manaus (improved scale) and simplified the physical and personnel structures (improving the process). Keeping the operations separate would entail a higher cost.
>
> *(Interview with the author, 2017)*

During the field research, TVChina had about 670 workers coming from a manufacturing process that produces TVs, tablets, and monitors. From this total labor force, about 50 workers were from China, who, as occurred in the other companies researched, occupied management, coordination, and supervision positions in the factory.

It is also important to point out here that researcher Izabel Valle (2007) conducted studies in this factory between 1998 and 1999, when the company still belonged to the Dutch group. According to the author, in December 1997, the company had 2,128 employees. Such a significant reduction in labor was due to the automation process implemented in the 1990s. The factory started to assemble the final product only and no longer produced the inputs which caused the layoff of many workers at the time of the acquisition by Chinese capital.

Import Management System

One of the basic elements of the Chinese companies' operations in the Manaus Free Trade Zone is the import of inputs from headquarters, meaning that the HR sector, the production organization, the process, and the management operate around it and are affected by it. Therefore, there is a dependence on imports in all other spheres of production in the Manaus Industrial Park, which prevents strong links from being created in the production chain and in the local social relations.

I call this configuration "Import Management System", the result of the "Chinese gravitational force" over the various productive territories, to use an expression by Pires (2009: 100), in order to take control of the global input production chain.

A large part of what the companies surveyed, manufacture in Manaus, has China as the origin of the components and raw materials. This means an average of 85% of what is required to make the final product. In fact, this has already been pre-manufactured in CKD (Completely Knocked Down) kits that, once in Manaus, are assembled using what the Brazilian legislation demands as a minimum content of local production: the Basic Productive Process (PPB).[8]

Table 3.1 shows the percentage of local, national, and international inputs in the surveyed companies, showing the dependence on imports.

These inputs from China arrive in Manaus by river, in ships that take about 60 days to dock in the city's ports. This delay, according to some interviewees, is due to the "cabotage" shipping process. The final destination of ships coming from China is ports along the Brazilian coast, requiring the transfer of the supplies to other ships. From there, they continue along the Brazilian coast, enter the mouth of the Amazon River in the state of Pará, and sail on this river for days before reaching Manaus. We can exemplify this through Figure 3.1.

MotorChina's case exemplifies this process, which according to the company's industrial director:

> We have logistical problems, because in general our inputs are imported from China via the port of Santos, and then forwarded to Manaus. The finished product goes from Manaus to the city of Fortaleza, and then to the port of Suape, in the northeast, where it is shopped for resale. This takes time.
>
> *(Interview with the author, 2015)*

TABLE 3.1 – Input import by the researched companies (2010) (percent)

Companies	*Acquisition (%)*			
	Local	*National*	*Abroad*	*Total*
TVChina	4.85	0.31	94.82	100.00
China Board	8.17	3.39	88.43	100.00
MotorChina	6.87	8.87	84.24	100.00
ArconChina	13.49	7.79	78.70	100.00

Source: Statistics collected and compiled by the author.

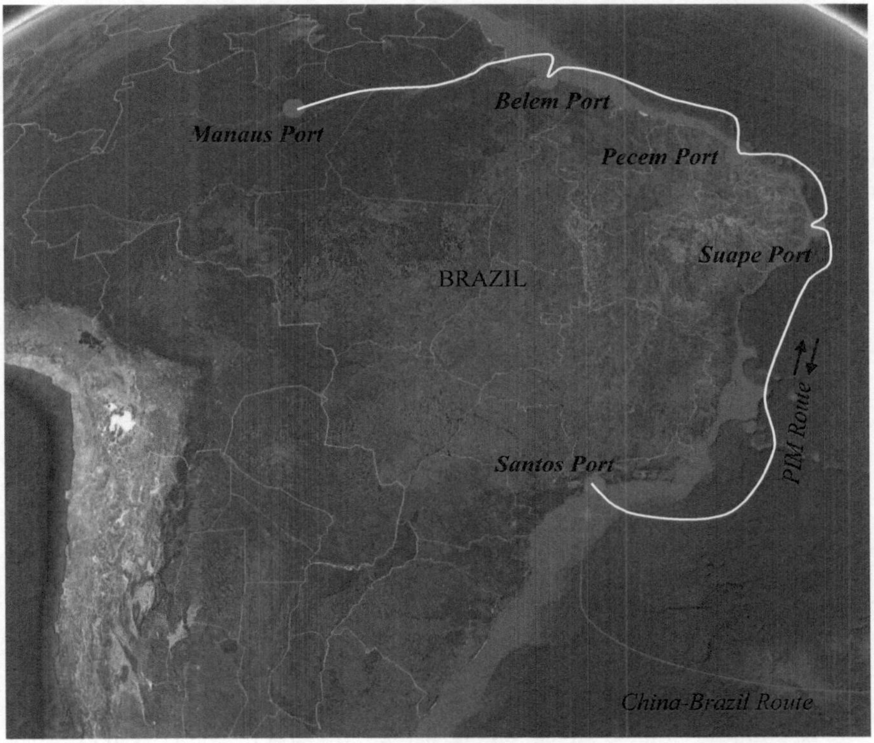

FIGURE 3.1 – The Tropical Silk Road and the Manaus Industrial Park Route

Source: Figure from Google Maps adapted by the author.

But if this takes time, why do Chinese companies prefer to bring inputs from China rather than buying from local suppliers[9]?

For MotorChina's board of directors, it is worth it because the cost is much lower when compared to the local similar. "Today, the main attraction of China is the cost. The Chinese are unbeatable in terms of cost. Nowadays, it compensates a lot to import both raw materials and finished products from China". A China Board engineer who stated that, for the company, it is not worth buying certain boards in Manaus, because the cost is higher when compared to Chinese-made boards, also shares the below view.

> Every factory can import material, but it must have a quota of material bought here in Brazil. Which boards are cheaper to make here? It is the motherboard, cheaper to make because it is a big board. IR board is a tiny little board, it's a board installed in a television set, I buy it from China, and it is cheap. A set of IR board in China cost two dollars. If we have one of these

> boards made here in Brazil it will cost about 10 dollars. Imagine a production of 10 thousand boards, 10 thousand televisions!
>
> *(Interview with the author, 2015)*

For a TVChina manager, it is not just a matter of lower costs but also a determination from the Chinese headquarters, which determines in advance what steps the Brazilian subsidiary should take:

> Everything is defined in China. They sell machines and kits to Brazil. Everything comes from China. Only a small percentage comes from here. Local purchases are much faster, but when the product comes from China, replacement time takes a long time, because if a shipment is delayed, it becomes a problem. We do not work with inventory, but with a three-month planning. We have a logistics system that controls purchases, the entire logistics. Through this system, China controls our inventory. The logistics management there determines what we will use in three months.
>
> *(Interview with the author, 2015)*

This whole import process has consequences on production insofar as it "sets the tone" for production. However, since there is no "just-in-time" supplier – because he is on another continent – it is necessary to build up inventory of inputs. In some companies, material is stocked for a month. In others, stocks are built up to two or three months.

In fact, for the Chinese capital, on one hand, a low-cost inventory is an essential part of the production process in Manaus. On the other hand, this creates a logistical dependency that does not allow for a Japanese-style production, that is, a production driven by demand and not by inventory, thus creating a double implication for the Chinese factory: a shortage or surplus of inputs. Therefore, it is necessary for human resources and production sectors to come up with strategies that transform the unforeseen into profit or, at least, mitigate possible losses.

When there is a surplus of inputs, a strategy adopted is to sell them to other local companies or even export them. The sale of inputs occurs not only when there are surpluses but also when there is disposal of those that arrive defective from China, as small companies in the PIM end up using discarded materials (scrap),[10] and that turns into a profit opportunity for the Chinese factories. One interviewee described how this system works:

> Very heavy supplies come by ship and sometimes it takes a month, forty days, to get here. So, a planning sector does this control. This ends up creating inventory because, often, the client cancels the order. . . . When there is too much inventory, we can sell this material in the Manaus Free Trade Zone; others, we export. . . . This is something done quite often. They say it is because the order was canceled, but in fact, the company imports too much and leaves the material there, without use.
>
> *(Interview with the author, 2014)*

In addition to measures such as those mentioned earlier, another strategy adopted by Chinese factories has been to reduce the workforce when the amount of inventory is higher than the product demand to be processed. A manager from MotorChina pointed out to me a situation that happened in 2014:

> We have been working with inventory for a month. This year, due to lower sales, we were left with a bit too much stock. Therefore, we had to give the staff time off, to avoid excess inventory. Then, we reduced the lines' production capacity and had to lay off workers. During the first semester, we were producing 2,800 motorcycles per month. Our production used to be 150 to 170 motorcycles a day. By the second half of the year, things changed. Moreover, to avoid too much inventory, I had to reduce the capacity of the line from 150 to 100. With that, there were too many people, so we had to remove some workers, namely from the factory floor.
>
> *(Interview with the author, 2014)*

However, in the event of small inventory in the factory and long delays in ship logistics, we have to literally stop production, as explained by an engineer from the TVChina company:

> Once we stayed at home for two weeks for lack of material because the supplies were late. So, what do you do in this situation? In this case, we had to wait for the supply to return to normal. Then our entire production was compromised.
>
> *(Interview with the author, 2014)*

In general, besides creating a logistical dependency and pointing out the local industry's need and vulnerability, in its micro spectrum, the import management causes a rework in the Chinese factories at ZFM. According to one interviewee, the Chinese send the inputs without making a rigorous selection of which components are defective, because they think it is cheaper to repair them in Manaus than to have them fixed right there in China.

Therefore, when the components arrive at the factories in Manaus, the defective ones that can be repaired are repaired and then used in the production process. Consequently, Manaus, works as a "workshop", where parts not complying with the quality standards of the companies are reworked.

Since almost all components are imported, what is actually used as a local component is the minimum required by the PPB. In the case of TVChina, these components include the packaging bag, styrofoam, box, user instruction manual, Wi-Fi card, power cable and labels. As for MotorChina, the items supplied locally are the tires, the transmission crown, transmission pinion, rearview mirror, reflector, side stand, wheel spacers, and brake rod. In China Board, local suppliers provide some printed circuit boards, wiring, and welding.

In this discussion between what is local and what is imported, there is a conflict of interests involving factories and control agencies. If PPB is too flexible, then those who criticize the ZFM model have reason, because many say that Manaus does not have a complex industrial process, only imports and assembles. If it is rigid, the factories may seek other productive territories more advantageous to their interests. One can say that, in this situation, government agencies end up being critical of imports, but, in practice, they give in to a production model that has imports as its basic structure, as happens with Chinese capital.

According to import managers, the Chinese head office monitors very closely the "quota" of products that must be local and those that can be imported. Therefore, at the Manaus plants, there is a specific sector that deals with PPB and that is directly subordinated to China, demanding that both Brazilian and Chinese workers send reports on the status of the local legislation. The person responsible for this area in one of the companies (PPB analyst) addressed this issue:

> We have to submit a weekly report on the processes being monitored, the ones in progress, and those which are not. Since we deal with products at PPB, we list the products that are active and the ones that are not. The active ones are those being manufactured in the company, the inactive ones are projects that are interrupted. Therefore, every week we have to send this feedback to headquarters, pointing out what can be imported and what cannot.
>
> *(Interview with the author, 2014)*

It is worth noting that even those items that would be considered "local" production also come from China, such as TVChina, which uses printed circuit boards that are theoretically local, but as the company's Human Resources manager shows, the supplier also imports most of the components:

> Here we buy the assembled printed circuit boards from a local supplier, which in turn imports 95% of the components it uses in its production process. That is, that percentage depends on which part of the production chain your business is in. Intermediate goods tend to have a higher percentage of imports than final goods.
>
> *(Interview with the author, 2014)*

Taking this into account, the import percentage in the companies researched is higher than it appears to be, since many of the local suppliers are also large importers from China, thereby creating a kind of "camouflage" within the PPB itself. More than this, importing most of its inputs promotes a *heavy factory*, with inflexibility and rigidity in the production organization. Working with up to three months of inventory and the delay to see the results of actions taken by the management exemplify this. The statement of this manager from ArconChina goes in this direction:

> Product lead times can take months. Therefore, it may take a few months for our Manaus factory to adjust to a sudden market variation, meanwhile the company absorbs all losses from a high inventory or an opportunity loss.
>
> *(Interview with the author, 2017)*

That is what happened in 2015. In 2014, when I conducted field research, TVChina employed about 800 workers. In September 2015, during another visit to the factory, the company was employing about 1,500 workers, which surprised me, given the economic difficulties faced by the country and the Brazilian domestic market retraction. However, as the HR manager made clear, TVChina was not moving in the opposite way as most industries. It was in fact correcting a planning error arising from this relationship with a production "pushed" by the input import system and had to hire more people after adjusting its input inventory:

> In 2014, right after the sales for the FIFA World Cup (April and May 2014), the company predicted that the market would drop and adjusted to get through the difficult time by reducing 4 production lines. . . . The forecast was correct, but the size was wrong. We made more cuts than necessary, which only became apparent in September 2014. However, with a 4-month inventory of materials, it would no longer be possible to adapt to the correct scenario. So, we held the level we were at and, at the beginning of this year (2015), we hired three more production lines, increasing the number of employees and returning to normality.
>
> *(Interview with the author, 2015)*

In addition to pointing to one of the characteristics of the Chinese production model in Manaus, the import management observed in Chinese companies is also a means to visualize the current functioning of PIM. The acquisition of inputs abroad has been increasing since the early 2000s, especially in the electrical and electronics subsector, driven not only by Chinese companies but also by other international factories.

Nevertheless, when analyzing the general picture of acquisition, Chinese capital showed above-average imports, especially in the electrical and electronics subsector, which, between 2010 and 2015, bought from abroad 77% of its input needs for production. The situation is similar in the mechanical subsector, where the factory surveyed imported almost 80% of its inputs, while the subsector imported just over 50%. Compared to a competing European air-conditioning plant, imports made by the Chinese accounted for 78.70% against 51.71% by European companies.

The biggest difference was found in the two-wheeler subsector. While the percentage of foreign purchases from this subsector was around 43.42% in 2015, MotorChina presented almost 85%. Compared to a Japanese competitor, there is a considerable contrast, as the latter purchases less than 20% of its inputs externally. Table 3.2 depicts this reality.

The fact is that, in this scenario, one perceives a production pattern primarily focused on input imports, with Chinese capital being the leading player in this production practice. Far from the Japanese philosophy, which advocates the use of just-in-time manufacturing operations, the Chinese production model does not consider it one of its fundamental concerns in Manaus, because imports function as part of their overseas factories' coordination and behavior.

TABLE 3.2 – Acquisition of inputs by the major PIM companies (2010) (percent)

Company	*Country*	*Product*	*Purchases of inputs (%)*			
			Local	*National*	*Abroad*	*Total*
TVChina	China	TVs, monitors, and tablets	4.85	0.31	94.82	100.00
China Board	China	Boards	8.17	3.39	88.43	100.00
iFexx	China	Boards	2.42	0.00	97.57	100.00
Bomoong	South Korea	TV	8.32	1.32	90.47	100.00
NNG	South Korea	TV	7.84	1.54	90.60	100.00
Zonic	Japan	TV	11.29	0.33	88.37	100.00
Hunamo	Japan	TV	4.55	1.83	93.60	100.00
Climexx	USA/China	Air-conditioning	15.36	1.73	82.89	100.00
ArconChina	China	Air-conditioning	13.49	7.79	78.70	100.00
Eurogreen	Sweden	Air-conditioning	22.05	26.23	51.71	100.00
MotorChina	China	Motorcycles	6.87	8.87	84.24	100.00
Hamayda	Japan	Motorcycles	50.60	28.23	17.16	100.00
Subsector	**Average purchases abroad (2010–2015) %**					
Electronics	77.67					
Two-wheelers	33.81					
Mechanical	56.45					

Source: Statistics collected and compiled by the author.

In this external operation, some of its *raisons d'être* stand out. First, the importation of inputs creates a demand for expatriates in Manaus, something that interests the parent company, because they cost less than Brazilian managers would, as we will see later. Furthermore, the Chinese deals directly with inventory control and operates the logistics involved from China to Manaus. Therefore, there is a harmony between these two Chinese model systems: input imports by the subsidiaries and the expatriation of workers by the headquarters.

Second, the import of inputs is part of the Chinese capital's expansion strategy, that seeks to flood the global markets with competitive prices and advanced technology and that includes not only the final product but also raw materials, machinery, and equipment used in production, something that occurs in Manaus today. More important is that such a system means controlling the production chain of goods and inputs, thus creating a dependency that is supplied by Chinese export factories.

This last aspect shows another dimension of this system, namely, to meet a demand from Chinese exporting companies that want to participate in China's current "going outside" moment. This is a phenomenon seen on several continents, especially among contractors who benefit from Chinese government contracts to build infrastructure in several countries. In the case of the manufacturing sector and faced with a class of input producers with idle productive capacity, China's internationalized factories play the role of creating external demand for one of the most important domestic sectors of the country's economy.

Therefore, input imports and the inventory policy in the Chinese factories are considered as planning and as a competitive advantage. Not as a cost – something seen in the Japanese management philosophy – even though this, as emphasized, may generate some setbacks and logistical mishaps. In a China that controls both the production process and the logistics and input sales, planned inventory and imports emerge, however, it does not allow factories to create local production and technological processes.

Chinese enclaves: the Human Resources policy of the companies

In the surveyed companies, it is worth noting that the Human Resources sector responds directly and is subordinated to Chinese headquarters. This has meant that actions involving hiring, firing, training policies, qualification, salary issues, and worker benefits must first be reported to China, await a decision, and only then be implemented or halted.

Research done by Lee (2009) on Chinese corporations in Africa, and Čaněk (2016), Smith & Zheng (2016), and Sacchetto & Andrijasevic (2016) on Chinese presence in Europe, for example, indicate similar processes in these regions as a mean to control the local labor force.

There are similar, but also specific, aspects in Manaus. These elements I call "Human Resources of Chinese enclaves" have had an impact on the companies' manufacturing structure, on the organizational hierarchy, and on the functions of this sector. With regard to this last aspect, it is important to note that the local management of the factories has no influence over HR, which is entirely controlled by HR in China. The HR manager of the company ArconChina addresses this issue:

> We are in direct contact with the headquarters in China. The local Human Resources sector does not report to the director in Manaus. In fact, it is an independent function, a matrix organization. So, I do not report to the local director at all. Obviously, in a functional way, yes, I have to help him as a service provider. However, my manager, the one who decides my life, raises, promotions, etc. He is in China. He is the global human resources director; This is meant to grant more independence to the function, to make it easier for you to negotiate human resources issues with the company's management, otherwise it would be much easier for the company to cut this, cut that, change this, change that. . . . There are also other functions like that here, too. The information technology is like that, it also reports directly to the head office.
>
> *(Interview with the author, 2014)*

In practice, HR as a Chinese enclave decides the local affairs on a global basis. This makes not only the production more *Made in China* and less *Produced in Manaus* but also the institutions of the companies and their systems of mediation. Local HR as a "global Chinese territory" is thus part of how China coordinates and controls production in its current phase.

In addition to hiring workers and paying wages, for example, this sector has the function of giving China the power to decide both basic and more complex local issues, reporting them to the headquarters to be understood and decided on the other side of the world. Furthermore, it is a way to avoid dealing directly with the pressures of the place, putting them under the decision-making power of the China-based management.

This can be exemplified in issues involving labor disputes, since it is the Chinese headquarters that decides whether or not labor agreements made in Manaus should be signed, or if it is more beneficial for the corporation to pay a fine. In order to operationalize this process, the head office requests that the documents be sent to China, designates and chooses the Chinese who are in Manaus as witnesses in labor lawsuits, and builds a map of the lawsuits that are in progress or that are likely to be filed in the Labor Court.

A report by an HR manager helps to understand this situation:

> I receive annual goals sent by headquarters. They send them by telephone, teleconferences twice a year, videoconferences every week, teleconferences and e-mails daily. If they come up with a new policy, they present it, send it, and tell us what we have to adapt. Moreover, I have to report what is happening here. Every week there is a kind of weekly report indicating the main activities of the previous week, what was accomplished and the progress of the actions that they are already monitoring. This includes everything: number of hiring, number of people I have in the plant, both direct and indirect, the new labor lawsuits that may arise, *they control them all. They have a complete list:* the ones that had a hearing, what happened during the hearing, what was agreed, what was not agreed. In short, if the profit and result negotiation with the workers is going to happen. They are monitoring with us a labor union negotiation. Whatever separate payroll payments I have to make I must report to them. If I have an audit, an inspection from the Labor Prosecutor's Office, from the Regional Labor Agency. They want to monitor the results, if there was any action plan, any non-compliance, any recommendation for improvement, what we have to do, what is the action plan. They continue monitoring until the action is finally closed.
>
> *(Interview with the author, 2015)*

For this HR manager, the Chinese control over the Human Resources policies occurs "because they cannot understand the many Brazilian labor laws, and neither can they understand how the company has to deal with them". He said that in one specific occasion, a Chinese production manager wanted HR to call a worker who was on vacation from work. Therefore, he told the Chinese that the law did not allow it, but the manager refused to "conform and still wanted to call the employee and tell him to come back from vacation and go to work".

A similar view is shared by one manager from TVChina company and by one from the China Board. For the former,

> The Chinese cannot understand very well the strictness of the Brazilian labor legislation, namely, the amount of social contributions, overtime controls, the quotas set by the government to hire handicapped people. The Young Apprentice[11] program also has its quota for this. They cannot understand very well the rigidity in determining vacations. When you take vacation, the employee has no right, not even by himself, of not using, selling. He cannot access the company, because the vacation period is by law, you suspend the employee's contract, and it is as if he was not working for the company. The employee is strictly forbidden to come into the company during the entire vacation period. The Chinese cannot understand any of this.
>
> *(Interview with the author, 2014)*

To the second manager,

> One of the biggest difficulties faced by the Chinese is the difference between the Chinese and Brazilian labor laws. This poses a difficulty for those running the company as well as for the Chinese managers to understand all the obligations, and that failure to comply with them would make the business unviable in Brazil.
>
> *(Interview with the author, 2016)*

For an administrative assistant, what stands out in the Chinese relationship with HR is the control and demand for bureaucratic procedures. She explains her view as follows:

> In my department, the most obvious thing about the Chinese is control. They implement control at a very high level, even if this control means going back in time and using paper for approvals. Everything is very bureaucratic, with stamps, etc. I myself, for example, have three different stamps to approve several things. It is a requirement of the Chinese company, a Chinese culture. The information systems are there, but they think that you cannot always control everything through the information system. Therefore, the Chinese really implement some paper controls to guarantee that everything is really controlled. Another thing about their culture is that they invest a lot in property security. That means you have guards everywhere, watching the assets.
>
> *(Interview with the author, 2014)*

In face of the different aspects of the parent–subsidiary relationship, and the various reasons that lead HR China to function as a Chinese territory within the PIM – many of which were highlighted by workers and managers, it is clear that we are before something specific to Chinese management, both in content and in scale, a different culture and factory standard from other foreign companies present in Manaus. In addition, it shows a view of the current Chinese globalization, which is strategically organized as an economic and bureaucratic block in other countries, forming a control and coordination system for the production, management, and Human Resources policies of its factories.

In addition to these elements, the relationship between factories and labor unions in Manaus has a conflictual backdrop and a search for adjustments that characterize the presence of Chinese capital in the city. According to the managers interviewed, the unions are no longer as "radical" as they were when the Chinese companies first arrived, but are more open to dialogue and do not want to stop the factories for whatever reason.

The report by the HR manager of one of the companies provides an illustration about this:

> Nowadays, the labor union no longer brings those impositions or radicalisms that existed in the past, 20, 30 years ago. Therefore, I believe that our relationship with the union today is very good, because they are more open. In fact, we have trade union directors who are also the company's employees, and they can come here whenever they want. If there is any employee complaint about the food in the cafeteria not being good, the union comes here, sits down with us, discusses, we check with the cafeteria staff to see what happened on that specific day of the complaint, we try to address the root cause, and so on.
>
> *(Interview with the author, 2015)*

Despite showing a greater relationship with the unions, this discourse contrasted with the position of some local union leaders, who emphasized the difficulty posed by the Chinese companies concerning union activities. In this line, the leaders pointed out that when the companies were first established, they would not allow representatives to circulate inside the factories or hand out leaflets to workers, barring them at the factory gate. There were also cases of dismissal of those who were more involved with the union. Afterward, with a greater confrontation and search for negotiations, this problem was remedied, but the Chinese continued to mistrust and prejudice labor union activity.

One approach found by HR to mitigate possible "estrangements" between Chinese workers and employees was to offer good manners courses and lectures given by labor lawyers for the new arrivals in Brazil. According to a manager, offering this type of training course sought to educate the Chinese on Brazilian laws, and how they should behave at work, because in some situations, "there has already been harassment with employees, that sort of thing". We also tried to emphasize the importance of Labor Justice in Brazil, which, according to the manager, is considerably more favorable to the workers' claims.

The strategy has yielded results, although limited. The Chinese interviewees praised the Brazilian legislation and trade unions. For example, they stated that the local union leadership, unlike the unionism in China, did in fact protect the Brazilian workers. But, they continued to think that Brazil has many labor benefits, good for the worker and bad for the Brazilian development. They also emphasized that many union leaders were only in office due to job stability, guaranteed to them by law, and "by not working, showing up at the plant only when they want to" (Interview with the author, 2016).

Summary

This chapter has highlighted the Chinese path toward the southern part of the world, which has positioned Brazil as its main object in South America, with Chinese interests and investments in all regions of the country. The Amazon stands out in this scenario as a target for Chinese ambitions due to its natural resources, minerals, and energy potential, also because it has a manufacturing structure with cheap and specialized labor located in the Manaus Free Trade Zone, the gateway to the domestic market for manufactured goods.

It was within this scenario that the Chinese factories landed in the region, promoting a mixture of fear and euphoria among the local public and private leaderships, while fostering deep changes in the way factories were organized and in the relationship with workers. In the first aspect, the field research showed that imports from China function as the main basis of Chinese capital's production methods by creating a dependence on machinery and inputs to be supplied by the country's exporting companies. It also evidenced that the factories' HR is systematized as a *Chinese enclave*, in order to bring China's bureaucratic/matrix control and management into the Amazon factory.

As for the second element, the "politicized" discourse of many union leaders about these factories was evident, even though they showed the Chinese unfamiliarity with Brazilian manufacturing reality, especially the labor legislation, something always presents in the words of Brazilian and expatriate managers.

In the face of this conundrum, the field research and the data analysis revealed that, in fact, the Chinese factories were in a mix of adaptation and a process of local labor insecurity. If in one aspect of the investigation, we could not see any "Chinese savagery" underway in Manaus, in another, we could see great difficulties by the Chinese in meeting workers' demands, especially in relation to wages, benefits, qualification, participation, and valorization of labor, creating a process of labor insecurity in the PIM, as we will see in the next chapter.

Notes

1 All of these projects have been highly contested locally, especially by the indigenous and riverside populations already affected or that may suffer material and cultural losses caused by these enterprises, as shown in the works of Moreno (2015), Aguiar (2017), and Oliveira (2018).

2 When compared with other states, in 2015, Amazonas represented almost 15% of Brazil's total imports from China. This rate was once higher, reaching 22% in 1997.

3 Direct employees, excluding temporary and outsourced workers.
4 The interviewee refers to critics about the Manaus Free Trade Zone that see it only as an assembly site for products, with no local industrial transformation process.
5 Andrijasevic & Sacchetto (2016: 350) point out that the installation of Chinese factories in Eastern Europe not only makes it possible to escape the high Eurozone tariff barriers but also allows the Chinese to manufacture products with the *Made in the EU* label instead of *Made in China*.
6 In that context, 30% of the TV brand belonged to the Dutch parent company while 70% belonged to the Chinese parent company.
7 In this case, similar to what Andrijasevic & Sacchetto (2016) observed about the Chinese factory in Europe, stamping a product "Made by the Dutch" was a means to conquer the market, which had high acceptance of the Dutch TV brand.
8 The Basic Productive Process (PPB in Portuguese) is a Brazilian regulation that determines a minimum set of operations at the manufacturing plant to measure whether a given product is being locally manufactured.
9 Some industrial directors justify the high percentage of imports by saying that local suppliers would not meet the factories' demand. According to these managers, even Brazil's southern and southeastern regions cannot meet the companies' demand for inputs. When one considers the tone of these managers' statements, a paradoxical question emerges regarding the country's own industrial policy: would there be no domestic suppliers because one imports too much, or would one import too much because there are no domestic suppliers?
10 In one of the factories investigated, there was an entire warehouse full of scrap, with materials such as components, manuals, semifinished products, cables, cancelled models, caps, and packaging boxes, among others.
11 Brazilian program for young students to access the labor market. Brazilian law determines that all large- or medium-sized companies must have 5%–15% apprentices among their employees, aged between 14 and 24 years and attending school.

4

HEAVY FACTORIES

The Chinese Production Model and its impacts on workers

Strong and weak ties among workers of PIM

As emphasized in Chapter 1 of this volume, between 2013 and 2017, I interviewed many different workers from different hierarchical levels and positions in the companies surveyed.

On average, these workers were about 33 years old. About 80% of them reported having worked previously in a PIM company, which places them as experienced Amazonian workers and trajectories associated with working in the Amazon's global factories.

Of the total, 75% of the interviewees were born in the city of Manaus. Others came from the Amazon hinterland, but there were also workers from neighboring states, such as Roraima and Pará.

When asked about the trajectory of their parents, most workers who declared they were born in the capital city of Amazonas responded that they had to "cross over" to Manaus in the 1970s and 1980s, moving from the countryside to Manaus. However, most of them are members of a "post-crossing" generation themselves. Together, parents and children can be considered the "working generation" of PIM – to use an expression of Lima & Conserva (2006) – and have undergone the inconsistencies and ups and downs of the world economy on a local basis.

One of these contradictions is the city's socio-spatial division, one of the richest in Brazil, but also one of the most unequal. This fact can be demonstrated by noting that most workers live in the city's periphery, in neighborhoods that, in most cases, were not planned, but results of squatting locally known as "invasion", that is, groups of people occupying an area without authorization and without help from the local government. Therefore, they can be considered to have a trajectory "between peripheries" and are enduring a precarious social mobility.

DOI: 10.4324/9781003229377-4

In terms of education, most of these workers finished high school and some of them were attending private colleges in Manaus. This is important to highlight, considering the level of education registered in the early 1990s – when more than half of the workers in the PIM had only completed elementary school (Salazar 1992) – or the reality of the late 1990s and early 2000s – when, amid the dissemination of the so-called "quality culture", a high school diploma was required to be admitted into factories. The new profile of the workers shows a higher level of education and, in many cases, an increase in college education.

However, it is worth noting that the surveyed companies do not impose that as a "direct" requirement, especially when it involves assembly work. Higher education is another important means for workers attempting to gain some degree of qualification as a differential during recruitment in companies' HR departments. It is also an attempt for them to be qualified for other positions in the factory or to pursue jobs in different economic sectors, because, as many of them told me, being in the PIM is not an option, but a condition.

However, getting a college degree comes up against objective conditions that create a social barrier between desire and achievement, which helps to understand why most workers on the factory floor only have a high school degree as their highest level of education.

First, among the implied limitations, is the difficulty in obtaining the specific knowledge necessary to gain access to public higher education. Then, there is the income commitment involved in attending a private higher education institution (depending on the salary level, one can have one-third of one's salary allocated to college tuition). There is also the availability of time, because, when we add work and commuting time in a big metropolis like Manaus, it generally takes up about 12 hours of the worker's daily routine. Finally, there are uncertainties such as permanence in the job, meaning that the worker has to consider the possibility of attending college on a stop-and-go basis. If laid off, they need to put off or even drop out of the course.

Given this scenario, one element mobilized by workers has been the creation of a "space of the possible", in the words of Bourdieu (1996), creating paths to allow them to transit through the instability of factory employment in Manaus so that they can have some predictability and security in the local labor world. To do this, they make use of social bonds.

As shown by Lima & Conserva (2006: 73), social bonds resemble parallel structures to the bureaucratic organization and are "informal social networks established by individuals in their daily lives in a utilitarian way in their search for a job, in their maintenance, and in their occupational mobility", facilitating access to employment or reducing the time spent searching.

This helps to understand why more than 60% of the workers got their jobs in the Chinese company through "friends' referrals", that is, one worker helping another. In this network, the wider the range of contacts, the more information is obtained. For the workers in our research, strong ties and weak ties – in Granovetter's (1973) terms – are part of this network of social bonds, and the workers use either of them.

A fundamental characteristic of this network is its flexibility to adapt to the labor market variations and to the specific needs of those who are part of it. In 2014, for example, many workers used the network to leave the Chinese companies and work for other companies. However, in 2015, given the onset of the Brazilian economic crisis and the beginning of layoffs at PIM, the opposite movement occurred, with many workers calling on their contacts to join Chinese companies.

Many workers in this scenario, with privileged information about new openings and with contacts inside the factories, become the center of the network. Not coincidentally, during the interviews conducted with workers at the TVChina company, for example, it was common to hear about "worker x" who would be negotiating a promotion or salary increase for "worker y". With the emergence of instant messaging applications, this network is spreading rapidly and the "network-worker" is becoming more prevalent among the participants. Besides being a systematic way to enter or stay in a job, the network's social bonds also provide a mechanism for workers to construct an evaluation procedure about work in factories, mapping which are the best and worst ones, those that pay the highest and lowest wages, offer the most and the least "benefits", etc. According to them, sometimes a company may have a lower salary, but the benefits may be higher than in another job, therefore, there is a form of rational calculation of the subjects that, by means of their subjective experiences and factory trajectories, can share on the network the paths to be pursued at the PIM.

While "informal" ties have meant an intense flow of information and experiences among workers, the same has not happened with "formal" ties. The Union leaders' attempts to attract the worker's attention, either by delivering a monthly newsletter at the factory door or by trying to get closer through the promotion of the union's mobilization actions on social networks, proved to be fragile and little referenced by the workers.

According to one union leader, this alienation between unions and workers is due, among other reasons, to less combativeness and the decline of direct action via "body-to-body" communication at the factory gate.

> Newsletter delivery at the factory gate has declined dramatically. In the past, we went to the factory, early and late in the morning or early and late in the afternoon, in other words, we showed up three times during the day and, afterwards, we would visit the associates and each one here had a task: "let us visit ten associates". So, you were supposed to go, you had this job during the month. Ten, fifteen, twenty members . . . you would talk to them, check how they were perceiving the union, the union management's actions, their complaints, and their relation with the factory and if the production process had increased. We monitored things very closely. That does not exist anymore.
>
> *(Interview with the author, 2016)*

For another union leader, the weak bonds between the union and the workers are not due only to the fact that the "face-to-face" at the factory gate is no longer intensively done, but rather to these leaders' failure to understand that there is a new type of worker:

> If the union leader arrived at the factory gate and said: "People, this is the situation: we are going through this, we are only eating sardines and eggs". It would inflame the entire factory and really stop everything. Not today. You take a young person and tell him: "Hey, you are eating only eggs!" He looks at you and says: "What does this guy have against eggs? It's so good with beans!" So, he has a different conception. You used to create a situation, inflamed the group' minds very easily. Not today. You must be very careful during a speech. Besides, today's youth does not accept being led too much. Therefore, it is difficult to foster participation. However, this is a situation all Unions experience nowadays all over Brazil, not only here in Amazonas.
>
> *(Interview with the author, 2015)*

Given the difficulty to attract workers using only the Union newsletter and the social networks, union leaders sought to adopt as a strategy the availability of transport to take workers to the union's headquarters and then leave them at home. When the expected result was not achieved, they started to use post-meeting attractions, such as offering snacks and drinks. A different union leader relates the following:

> Our leaders demand: "Look, we have to invite the people, but there has to be a beer". Then the guy, who is also involved in this culture, when invited to the assembly, he says: "But will there be any beer for us? If not, I won't go, because today is Friday. I will see". He says he will go, gives an excuse, but doesn't show up. And if you look at an assembly called here, 70% of the workers only go because they have transportation, a snack – because we still give a snack to the people – and because before they leave, there's some beer for the people.
>
> *(Interview with the author, 2015)*

In addition to those elements pointed out by the leaders who help to explain the fragile bonds between workers and unions, others corroborated this alienation process. The 1990's corporate restructuring introduced managerial methods to keep the union away from the companies, either through the so-called "worker participation and collaboration policy" or through a preventive Human Resources sector that anticipated labor union action.

As shown by Humphrey (1995), the arrival of this new Japanese-inspired management method introduced management tricks in Brazilian factories, based on the policy of bonuses, rewards, and "breakfast with the boss" for workers who participated in the plant management by giving ideas and getting involved in management projects.

> Companies often associate union activities with militancy and resistance to changes. Fearful of worker militancy, they are eager to keep unions away

> from the factories. One way to achieve this is to anticipate union demands by offering wages and working conditions that are attractive to workers.
>
> *(Humphrey 1995: 134)*

Ramalho (1997) indicated that the productive reorganization expressed a business community's "ideological imposition" without gains for the working class. In turn, he argued that there was a search to "capture the subjectivity" of the workers. When discussing how this process occurred in Manaus in the late 1990s, Valle (2007: 82) noted that

> The total quality programs and/or forms of participative management started to be widely disseminated because the idea currently in use that the "human factor" is the decisive element in the productive process. Therefore, they encouraged "partnership" between workers and company, improved communication between the different levels of the hierarchy, and worker commitment to quality and productivity. "Production teams", "production cells", "production units", "suggestion boxes" have become widely used. Participation was encouraged through bonuses, prizes and/or profit sharing.

As a result, the companies gradually attracted workers and the relationship with the unions became more distant. The following statement from a worker in the MotorChina company shows the current dimension of this process:

> Whenever people needed anything, they asked Human Resources for help, and they intervened. I personally never requested anything from the union.
>
> *(Interview with the author, 2016)*

Giving a similar assessment, another interviewee told me this:

> The only thing I see the Union doing is to communicate holidays, how many days we are going to work during the week, communicate those days off that we had. "You are going to take a week off. You will get paid on the day off, but you will have to work on Saturday. Then, in the exchange, it will be 2 for 1: 2 days off for 1 day of work". I don't know exact role of the union there in the company.
>
> *(Interview with the author, 2016)*

The workers also gave other explanations for their low level of involvement with the union, for example, "They only sign the agreements made with the company"; "they go there and rubber stamp the factory's interests. They are more favorable to the boss than to the employees"; "I don't really see them acting"; and "I've never seen them in the factory". On the other hand, there were workers who, despite stressing not "wanting involvement with the union", highlighted its role in defending the interests of the working class:

> They also act like this: if there is a complaint against a company, they confront the company. When a complaint is made regarding a lack of work safety, they even look at ergonomics and work safety. The union also analyzes this, when you are fired from a company, the union also analyzes this to see if the company is giving you the right compensation The union is the employee's father when it comes to guaranteeing the employee's rights. However, I am not a union member. I never was, I never liked it.
>
> *(Interview with the author, 2016)*

Another important component that explains the fragile bonds between unions and workers today is the representation crisis that has hit Brazil caused by the labor reform approved by the Brazilian Congress in 2017. Among the many changes, the one that affected mostly the workers' representation was the end of the annual compulsory union tax. This tax was an important source of funds for the organization of these unions; the obligation for workers who lose lawsuits against the company, to bear the legal costs inflicted at the Labor Court[1]; and permission for outsourcing, remote work, and the worker as a "legal entity". These measures divided the workforce into several subgroups and made the job representation of these new categories a challenge still unsolved by Brazilian trade unions.

The law is the limit: wage and labor benefits policy[2]

Chinese investment in Manaus factories has been below the amounts spent by other companies in terms of salaries and benefits, or not progressing beyond the legal minimum. It also shows little involvement with worker qualification policies, leaving this responsibility to the individuals themselves. This is in line with international authors who indicate Chinese difficulty in terms of better wage payments in various parts of the globe (Burgoon & Raess 2014; Andrijasevic & Sacchetto 2016; Smith & Zheng 2016; Lee 2017).

Nevertheless, there are specific issues that deserve to be considered. One of them is the companies' policies seeking to pay a salary in the subsidiaries close to the average amount paid in the Chinese headquarters. In TVChina in Manaus, the operator received an average of US$476.00, while in China, US$590.00. At ArconChina, we have US$571.00 for the Manaus operator and US$780.00 for the headquarters operator. Finally, at MotorChina, subsidiary and parent company paid the operator US$640.00 and US$800.00, respectively.

These differences in wages are due to the economic transformations occurring in the Asian country in recent years. One major factor is the increase in wage levels, especially in the Chinese "public sector", whose average wages have been higher than salaries paid by the private sector. For comparison, note that in 2015, the average wage in urban units was about 40% higher than the average private sector wage in China, jumping from just over US$150.00 in 2003 to over US$600.00 in 2015.

This helps explain why salaries in the surveyed companies are higher in those that are located in *urban units*,[3] such as ArconChina and MotorChina.

About this China's wage evolution, says a Chinese worker who was interviewed, "The wage in China has changed a lot recently. Before it was very low[4]; now it is not". And he adds,

> The salary is even higher than the one in Manaus if you add workers' overtime. Because it her it is different from China. The amount varies a lot. Here in Brazil, you can only do two hours of overtime in one day. During two weeks, you can only have one Saturday of overtime. But not in China, my friend. There, in China, you have overtime every day. In addition, there is not much time off in a month. There is this kind of thing. So, when the operator does a lot of overtime, he reaches a very high level of salary.
>
> *(Interview with the author, 2016)*[5]

However, it is important to point out that this relationship between headquarters and subsidiary salaries cannot only take into account the salary itself, because the Chinese do not have a quota of social benefits that exists in Manaus. When this is added up, according to the Chinese and Brazilian managers interviewed, the difference between the salary of Manaus and China decreases.

The fact is that, when compared locally, Chinese factory wages in Manaus are generally below what is paid by other foreign companies in the PIM. The TVChina company paid an average monthly salary of US$1,032.00 in 2015. Taking into account a comparison with other companies in the same subsector, this Chinese plant had an average salary slightly above the salary levels of both a Japanese plant and two South Korean plants included in the comparison. However, when labor benefits are included in the analysis, Japanese companies were the ones that spent the most on this type of resource.

It is important to note that this lower percentage spent on labor benefits was already being practiced when TVChina started its operations in Manaus. As an example, in 2010, while the average monthly benefit at TVChina was about US$127.00, at the Dutch-owned factories, it was US$285.00. Despite this, TVChina pays an average salary above the average paid by the electronics subsector, which is US$782.00.

On the other hand, China Board had an average monthly wage of US$597.00 in 2015 which is below the average paid by other companies in the electronics subsector whose wage profile was analyzed, as well as the subsector as a whole. The volume allocated to labor benefits was also lower than that of other factories, including a Chinese competitor, with US$271.00 per worker.

ArconChina presented two different variables. Of the three air-conditioning manufacturing companies, the Chinese company paid the lowest average monthly salary, US$ 805.00. However, it was the one that spent the most on labor benefits for each employee, totaling US$414.00 per month. Furthermore, it had a higher average salary than the average paid by the mechanical subsector, which amounted to US$773.00.

In the two-wheeler subsector, the difference in remuneration between Chinese and other foreign companies was greater. For example, in 2015, MotorChina had a lower average monthly salary than other Chinese companies or a multinational of Japanese origin. While this figure in MotorChina was around US$657.00, in the Japanese company, it was almost three times higher, around US$1,655.00 per month. It is important to note that MotorChina's average salary was also below the average of the two-wheeler subsector (around US$ 1215.00). Meanwhile, the amount spent on benefits by MotorChina totaled US$411.00, against US$641.00 by the Japanese company, as shown in Table 4.1.

Breaking down the salaries in the investigated companies, one observes a trend that has been worsening since the 1990s, when lower salary ranges began to represent a larger share of the total remuneration paid by the factories in Manaus. This has had more repercussions in the electronics subsector than in the two-wheeler subsector, where the predominant wage ranges have been above 1.5 minimum wages over the years.

Among the subsectors, on a case-by-case basis, some important variations are observed, such as a South Korean television manufacturer, which had almost 50% of its workforce earning between two and four minimum wages per month in 2015.

TABLE 4.1 – Average wages and benefits according to the company origin (2015) – (US$)

Company	*Country*	*Product*	*Monthly wage US$*	*Social benefits US$*
TVChina	China	TVs, monitors, and tablets	1,032.00	413.00
China Board	China	Boards	597.00	271.00
iFexx	China	Boards	734.00	348.00
Bomoong	South Korea	TV	902.00	862.00
NNG	South Korea	TV	820.00	384.00
Zonic	Japan	TV	1,043.00	444.00
Hunamo	Japan	TV	931.00	787.00
Climexx	USA/China	Air-conditioning	1,122.00	339.00
ArconChina	China	Air-conditioning	805.00	414.00
Eurogreen	Sweden	Air-conditioning	854.00	408.00
Fex Kongo	China	Motorcycles	996.00	255.00
MotorChina	China	Motorcycles	657.00	411.00
Hamayda	Japan	Motorcycles	1,655.00	641.00
Subsector	**Average wage of subsectors (2015) US$**			
Electronics	782.00			
Two-wheelers	1,215.00			
Mechanical	773.00			

Source: Statistics collected and compiled by the author. Company names are fictitious.

However, this is an exception to the rule. Most companies in the electrical and electronics subsector compared to one another actually have wage concentrations of up to two minimum wages. In addition, TVChina, China Board, and ArconChina follow this trend, by deepening them. In the latter's case, the percentage of workers earning up to two minimum wages per month was as high as 82% in 2015, while in its European competitor, this rate was around 50%.

In MotorChina, the amount of workers earning up to 1.5 minimum wages represented only 3.5% in 2015, while the 1.5 to 2 and 2 to 4 minimum wage ranges accounted for 47% and 37%, respectively. When comparing this Chinese company data with the Japanese firm's wage figures, also a motorcycle manufacturer, one notices that the high wages are more prominent in the Japanese company than in the Chinese one. For example, while at Motor China, the salary range with the highest number of workers was 1.5 to 2 minimum wages, at the Japanese company, it was 2 to 4. When it comes to workers earning between 6 and 10 wages, Motor China represented 4.5% and at the Japanese company, it was 11%.

The way Chinese factories in Manaus have been managing wages, benefits, and participation has had various implications on the lives of the workers interviewed.

Some of them mentioned that many of the benefits they received were higher in other companies and lower in the Chinese companies. Among them, the amount provided for food baskets was US$200.00 in Japanese companies and US$70.00 in Chinese companies. They also mentioned some benefits that they had in other companies, but which are either nonexistent in the Chinese management or accessible only through additional payment. For example, the dental plan, which in European companies was free, in the Chinese companies, they started charging US$7.00 per family member, deducted from the salary.

In addition, there were also salary reduction measures. A production operator from ArconChina reported, for example, that in his last job his salary was US$196, but that in the Chinese company his salary in the same position fell to US$170. A "backup"[6] worker also reported that the value of her salary was reduced when TVChina bought the Dutch company:

> In my position, I earned US$ 800.00, but in TVChina the amount was US$ 630.00. A supervisor was paid US$ 1700.00 in the Dutch company, and US$ 1190.00 in TVChina. There was also salary raises. In the Dutch company, whenever employees completed two years in the company, they would receive a letter congratulating them for being with the company for so long and saying that they would receive a US$ 10.00 raise the following month.
>
> *(Interview with the author, 2015)*

The case of the Dutch company's acquisition by TVChina characterizes well the transformations arising from the variation of global capital and evidences a process of labor precariousness in the Chinese factories in Manaus. An example of this is that many workers had their salaries lowered under the argument that they "earned too much" and that the management model of the old company was outdated, as a production leader told me:

> The Chinese said to us: "This company that you worked for was not a good one in terms of management. It is finished. Forget about it." . . . I heard this about five hundred times from the managers.
>
> *(Interview with the author, 2014)*

During the transition to the Chinese company, more than 70% of the workers who worked in the Dutch firm were fired – about 300 people – when the plant was sold to the Chinese. Months later, many of them were rehired, but with wages well below the ones, they earned before. Many labor benefits were also cut, among them were day care centers, milk aid, baby layette allowance, health plans, and the workers' savings fund.

> We had the following a policy there: we could deposit an amount in our account in the company and the company would deposit the same amount, too. If we left the company, we could redeem this amount. But the Chinese ended with our rights, they eliminated our leisure area, they closed the area destined for women, giving preference to men, they also closed the part of the area where we used to rest and watch TV and transformed it into production And many people who were employed by the Dutch company they sent away. They really cleaned it up.
>
> *(Interview with the author, 2014)*

Another interviewee also described this "Chinese dismantling":

> Before the sale, the company had a beauty parlor. The hairdresser would stay there to have our haircut. There was a room like a lan house, with several computers. There was also a library, some sofas with armchairs, you could read, if you wanted. You could stay on the Internet. It was 20 minutes for each employee, if they wanted. There was pool table, videogames, snacks, game room, trophy room for the tournaments we played, and a clothing store. The Chinese did away with everything. They broke everything and made an all-male lounge, because they give preference to men. Only the game room was left. They took away the lunchroom that sold popsicles, salad, cake, candy.
>
> *(Interview with the author, 2016)*

In addition to these elements, the interviews revealed that under the old company there was certain stability in employment associated with wage gains, bonuses, and labor benefit concessions. All that changed with the switch to Chinese companies, causing more turnover, absenteeism, and low wages, as reported in this testimonial:

> Some people there had been for with many years in the company. Because the Dutch had this thing about keeping their employees, they didn't fire them so easily, they tried to keep them. Therefore, there were employees who had been working for 15, 20, 30 years and were fired when TVChina took over. My supervisor had been in the company for 20 years, it was her first job; she started as an operator and became a supervisor. However, she was fired after The Chinese took over.
>
> *(Interview with the author, 2014)*

In this regard, a Brazilian manager described what the Chinese philosophy would be in relation to TVChina's labor expenses and noted what changes occurred with the arrival of the new company:

> One of the aspects of Chinese culture is, of course, that it is more aggressive in terms of expenses than the Dutch were. They had, in my understanding, a culture of accruing many employee benefits. Not the Chinese. They are very careful about the organization's expenses. Therefore, they do not concede benefits, contributions other than those that are required by law. Those that are required by law, yes, but those that are not required by law they question, and then start taking away.
>
> *(Interview with the author, 2014)*

He adds,

> For example, the Dutch company used to provide day care for 100% of the employees that needed to place children in a day care center. However, if you check the Brazilian law or even the collective labor convention, which is the one that complements this, it does not force you to give 100%. It doesn't demand it, it leaves a margin so you can meet within a specific quota. Therefore, the Chinese go after this quota. They do not understand that they have to give 100%. The law doesn't require it, there is no collective agreement, there is nothing, no requirement that demands it. So, they give what is fair, what has been defined. If in the following year the authorities decide that it has to be increased, they will comply, as long as there is specific quota, then that is the quota that they will meet. Therefore, it goes more or less like this. For example, there is a factory where managers receive a car every three years as a benefit. For the Chinese it is like this: "Is there a legal imposition"? "No!" "Then cut it, there is no need".
>
> *(Interview with the author, 2014)*

In this "cost cutting" and cost reductions used by international companies, it is important to stress that, besides the precariousness and losses for the labor force as a whole, even those benefits that have continued to be offered by the researched factories have been conditioned to a range of compensations required from workers. The aim is to control, via HR, the workers' "commitment" to production.

For example, at MotorChina and ArconChina, the requirement was no absences and no sick leave on the worker's monthly record. At TVChina and China Board, such criteria – associated with no material waste – were also used as rules for workers' access to benefits agreed with the unions. The consequence is a management with a top-down decision profile, with goals and "quotas" defined by the Chinese management collective and that seeks to reproduce locally a more technical and routinized work.

Collective management and individual labor: the matrix Taylorism

In fact, another element that characterized this "clash" between the Chinese company and the Manaus workers was the little appreciation for their creativity, i.e., a Chinese difficulty to create opportunities for dialogue in the factory and making the worker more participative. This process contrasts with the managerial tricks implemented by the local factories, which emphasized the importance of teamwork and worker involvement, as I discussed earlier.

Despite the fact that this type of factory artifice has been introduced since the 1990s to bring workers closer to the company and away from the union, as we have seen, the workers also used this space to claim for improvements in their work environments and to obtain some labor benefits. It is, therefore, a relationship of control/consent – to use Burawoy's (1979) expression – but organized and under pressure by the workers, who began to see in participation opportunities for growth and greater gains, although punctual.

However, instead of a "production of collaborators" – as pointed out by Andrade (2014) about the Japanese factory in Manaus – the "production of operators" has emerged under Chinese ownership. Because of this, process demands a type of worker with a specialized profile with more "operational" and technical nature, subordinated to a centralized management from China and organized around the pressure and control of the head office, but without much room for bonds with the workers in the region. Hence, I call this phenomenon *matrix Taylorism*, in which the power of participation is concentrated in the hands of expatriate Chinese managers.

Certain characteristics were observed under this system that exemplify, on the factory floor, the Chinese approach toward the Manaus worker.

The first one relates to the fact that the factories paid little attention to "informal" benefits, which traditionally worked at the PIM. They were tools to motivate workers to better accept the productive processes of the factories, such as lunch at a restaurant for the production line with the best performance, raffles for defective products or those with damaged packaging, and increased value in the Profit and Result program. An interviewee commented on this:

> Aside from the recognition: trophy, photo of the employees of the line, all of this was there on the wall for the quarter. I liked it very much. . . . Here there is nothing, just a mug I won on Mother's Day.
>
> *(Interview with the author, 2015)*

Another employee also described this same system:

> These gifts were good because they encouraged us. Because we spent the whole day there, assembling, with almost no rest. This was an incentive for us. For example, on Children's Day, the company would give them gifts, as well as at the end of the year. There was the chat with the manager once a month. Whoever was picked went to talk to the manager and could ask him anything s/he wanted, if s/he was going to ask for a bill, salaries, etc. Every month we talked with a different area manager. I never saw this here in ArconChina, not really.
>
> *(Interview with the author, 2015)*

Furthermore, as far as worker participation is concerned, they reported that management offered few opportunities to workers' "ideas", either from the factory floor or from the technical levels. In their capacity as employees who experienced the work transformations occurred in the late 1990s and 2000s, many referred to the nonexistence of the so-called "participation programs", such as continuous improvement groups, that had been a characteristic feature of management in Manaus (Andrade 2014). According to a production leader from Motor China, meetings with the workers occurred only a serious problem occurred or when a director from headquarters visited the Manaus subsidiary. In addition, opportunities to contribute with their ideas or to improve processes were not encouraged.

> With the Chinese you can't say that something is bad, you have to do it anyway. They say: "The instruction came from China, you can't change it. You have to do it this way because the guy in China does it this way and it works there, so this is what you have to do here. It has to be like this, it can't be changed". Therefore, we have no freedom to change things, to give ideas, and then it gets bad. . . . It was as if they had pulled the rug from under our feet, everything changed, they say that there is no such thing as encouraging anyone to work; "those who want to work, work".
>
> *(Interview with the author, 2015)*

In line with what was previously mentioned – that the predominance of Chinese management in Manaus is in its collective/corporate aspect and that ideas creation is seen as a management prerogative – a production engineer informed me that Chinese managers only accept suggestions if they are made jointly with an expatriate and are approved and forwarded by him. A TVChina production leader related the following situation:

> The Chinese won't accept any improvement of the process you propose. Example: I used to present my action plan and they didn't pay much attention to me. But if a Chinese individual presents an idea, it takes on gigantic proportions and is accepted. So, I started to give them my ideas as if it was theirs, and they accepted it. Otherwise, they wouldn't accept any idea, neither from the operation employee, nor from engineering. I think they think that giving them ideas is an insult, because they think that it is their job to give ideas.
>
> *(Interview with the author, 2016)*

Additionally, there are few tools to evaluate workers' satisfaction. At MotorChina, the production manager informed, "there is a tool, but it serves only to know the level of customer satisfaction. For the workers, we have not adopted this level here yet". At TVChina, there is an annual survey. Nevertheless, for an interviewee, "there is no use because they just define the questions [the management], and then they forget". At ArconChina, there is also no evaluation tool and, according to the import manager, "in case of dissatisfaction, the employee can call the company or send an e-mail".

For the workers, this practice has created little motivation to work, because they do not feel that they are "valued" by the company. A statement from a production operator emphasizes this:

> They don't even say good morning, or give us the opportunity to give ideas. Managers don't like it when we give ideas and opinions to change our position, to improve something. There is no suggestion box, they don't give anything. This discourages us.
>
> *(Interview with the author, 2014)*

Finally, it also highlighted the little emphasis given by Chinese managers to the notion of teamwork or the formation of work teams. One explanation for this phenomenon is that Chinese management is organized around the collective/corporate aspect of expatriate managers and its production is focused on the individual work of workers.

As a result, many workers and production leaders interviewed reported that they do not feel comfortable with these new companies and their consequences on managerial methods. For example, they emphasized that in their trajectories they have always seen teamwork and the role of a production leader (that rose from to this position from the workers) as a fundamental part of the work, something that has become a "PIM standard".

It started with the job interview, when recruiters asked about the ability and competence to "work in a team", to the production process itself, where mutual responsibilities and bonuses were emphasized. In production, the role of the leader was the organization of work teams and worker "motivation". According to the

Chinese view, the leader is less a motivator or team builder and more a control and voice of the Chinese managerial collective, also playing a supervisory role.

A production leader interviewed reported this aspect to me as follows:

> In the companies I worked for before, there was a lot of team spirit; I could call everyone to work, to get together, in a good way. The best production line, the best team, was rewarded. Here at China Board, that does not happen; There is only a lot of pressure coming from management, a lot of pressure to do things, too many demands and they forget to build teams. So, it's just a lot of pressure to reach the goal and that's it. They tell us: "You have to do your work there and that's it".
>
> *(Interview with the author, 2015)*

Once these elements were in place, the field research showed the following: the idea of "teamwork", search for a "proactive", "participative", and "skilled" worker previously seen as a key element of the Human Resources policy and even of the manufacturing sector of the companies in the PIM – and the policy of "collaboration" do not stand out in the Chinese companies. What is more prominent is the strong pressure exerted by the headquarters for cost reduction and for managerial control of the labor force. This ends up creating stronger bonds with China than with Manaus and makes the work strongly Taylorized.

Therefore, in the surveyed factories, a "cold", routine, hierarchical management emerges, with a managerial rationality focused on the technical management of work and organized around production rather than management.

Professional qualification and growth opportunities

In terms of the required qualifications, the Chinese companies' HR departments usually give preference to workers with previous experience at PIM. For managers, this criterion is associated with the Chinese goal of reducing costs with employee training, so it is essential to hire workers already familiar with a production line, or who have at least a notion of how it works.

In the case of the MotorChina factory, a minimum of six months experience in the two-wheeler sector is a "cutoff" factor for joining the company. According to management, "the worker comes already well trained and there is no need for large investments", because what is done in the factory "is very similar to what is done in other companies".

It is interesting to note that the companies' Human Resources departments demand from production line workers not only physical abilities from workers but also dynamism and speed.

> The Chinese demand very high speed in execution. . . . It is an environment full of pressure for speed and dynamism, because they bring an idea that this is how it is in China, very fast. Moreover, if it works there, it has to work here too.
>
> *(According to a manager interviewed by the author, 2015)*

In terms of schooling, the companies' Human Resources emphasize that a high school diploma is fundamental for operations on the factory floor, showing that there is little qualification requirement for the tasks performed on the assembly lines. Therefore, we see a reproduction of what has been observed during the last two years at the PIM in terms of worker training and qualification.

In two of the factories surveyed, the composition of the workforce by education level was very similar. At the China Board factory, of the 400 or so workers, around 70% had a high school education, 7% had an unfinished college education, and 13% were college graduates. In addition, slightly more than 3% had not finished high school. Meanwhile, at TVChina, of the approximately 670 workers, 70% had a high school education, 4.5% did not finish high school, and 15% had a college degree.

In general, a high school degree has been working, for a long time, as a "cutoff mark" for a job at the PIM. In addition, there are almost no workers with incomplete high school education. To get an idea of the transformation that took place, in 1997, as pointed out by Valle (2007), in the Dutch company that preceded TVChina, only 7% of the workers had a college education, a rate that more than doubled, reaching 15% in 2016, under Chinese ownership. Furthermore, during her study, the researcher recorded that 24% had an incomplete high school education. In 2017, at TVChina, this educational level represented less than 5%.

Besides a complete high school education, the Human Resources sectors have been demanding that workers, especially production leaders and supervisors, have a basic knowledge of English. According to a manager, this is fundamental, because many machines are imported from China or transferred directly from headquarters to the subsidiaries in Manaus. Since training for their operation is done by Chinese technicians, and considering the large number of expatriates that permeate the factory, English would facilitate communication in the production process.

Another certification placed not only as an important qualification, but also as a mandatory requirement for hiring is the Basic Operational Training (TBO in Portuguese), a course that cost approximately US$90.00 in 2016. According to a manager, for companies like ArconChina, the course is crucial because

> The TBO's teaching program includes training in basic operations for a production process, such as the use of screwdrivers, activities such as inserting connections, routing wiring and cabling, manual welding, placing labels, packaging products, etc. Therefore, since 2013, we have included this requirement into recruitment and selection.
>
> *(Interview with the author, 2016)*

Moreover, according to a TVChina production manager, hiring workers with basic assembly line training facilitates the ramp-up, that is, the learning curve that the assembly line with new operators or new products will have until it reaches its maximum performance. "Before the introduction of this training, we used to have a ramp-up of ten days. After TBO, it is possible to ramp up in just 3 to 4 days", explains the manager. He adds,

> Today, the production of this product begins with a new team. Then, the initial production goal of this crew is two thousand devices. Today, it will produce one hundred; tomorrow, three hundred; the day after tomorrow five hundred; then one thousand; until they reach two thousand. Because it requires that it creates efficiency to be able to streamline, so, in a speed pointed out by productive engineering, that a person is capable of producing in 10, 15 seconds a product or place the component there.
>
> *(Interview with the author, 2016)*

Largely, this HR policy reflects a way of taking production rationalization outside the factory. However, more than that, it reveals an attempt to transfer to the worker the responsibility for "qualifying" and "recycling in the market". During the interviews done with production and HR managers of the Chinese companies, it became evident that TBO, as soon as the Chinese investors arrived, was offered inside the factories themselves, free of charge, as part of the companies' training programs.

In order to reduce costs, HR started to require this training during the recruitment process as a prerequisite. In addition, even those workers with manufacturing experience, who had worked for some time on the assembly line, were required to take a course of this nature. One worker interviewed who had been fired and trying to be rehired in the same factory, observed:

> I've been through all interviews; I've taken the test. Only I must have this TBO, which they are now requiring. You will have a week of lecture and study on electronic components and stuff. Then you have to take a test to see if you approved.
>
> *(Interview with the author, 2014)*

Because of this requirement for new courses, it is evident that the companies began to benefit from a qualification at the workers' own expense, differently from previous years. It has also meant a change in the age workers start working in factories. Unlike in the 1990s, this has shifted from 18–20 years old to 22–25 years old.

If, on the one hand, training for the factory operational areas has been sought and paid by the workers themselves, due to the importance is given by the Chinese to the Engineering process and automation areas, on the other hand, the head office requires that Chinese managers train the Brazilian engineers to increase their skills and mathematical reasoning, which, according to them, was something that the local factories did not do quite often.

Nevertheless, many workers reported that despite having up-to-date qualifications, many obstacles are placed in their way to access the highest paid positions in the factories. The most important of these is that few growth opportunities are given to Brazilian workers in the company, since the top positions are largely held by Chinese, who end up favoring other Chinese. Also, according to them, a higher hierarchical level means a higher salary, which by no means interests the head office, which pays the Chinese a lower salary than a Brazilian would receive for the same position.

Changes in the organization form of work process

In general, the Chinese factories are replicating production trends that have already been underway since the late twentieth century at PIM.

Among these reproductions or their intensification, we list: a) the automation and miniaturization process of components, especially in the electro-electronic industry, a segment where high-tech machines and robotics are more widely used; b); limited requirement for higher skills in the operations, consisting mainly of repetitive tasks and "simple assembly" of equipment. The two-wheeler sector is the one with the most complex processes, using more technical work and the one that requires mechanical skills; c) reduced use of female labor, around 40%, compared to more than 60% in the 1990s, a change brought about by the intensive use of new production technologies, such as robotic machinery; and d) continuity of gender-segmented jobs, with women occupying lower paid positions and seen as "less qualified".

As far as the Chinese characteristics are concerned, a major one concerns the configuration of the assembly lines in the factories in Manaus. This happens because they were transferred from China to the Amazon, and had to be adapted to the Brazilian worker's biotype, who is taller than the Chinese workers. In addition, the machines had to be adjusted to match the local worker's speed, because, according to one interviewee who was a manufacturing manager at TVChina, "production lines in China run at a higher speed than in Brazil mainly to avoid chatter among workers and increase productivity".

Another element visualized in the research field was the great emphasis given to the engineering area of the factories. If, in the 1990s, this sector saw a decline in activities due to an increase in the import of pre-assembled kits, the Chinese factories reactivated many of their old functions, transferring the engineering system from their headquarters to Manaus. However, this reactivation was based mainly on reactive engineering rather than on technology developed at PIM itself.

For example, in China Board and TVChina, despite the existence of a New Product Introduction (NPI) and a Quality Engineering department, the research showed the inexistence of new products development or the strict control of production processes. Instead, the engineering areas were more concerned with the adequacy to the minimum industrial process required by the PPB, the local implementation of technologies and processes developed at headquarters, and repair of parts used in production, called by the workers themselves as the "repair sectors", functioning as local sorting of the inputs imported from China.

This also has to do with the fact that the machines and lines are imported, meaning that the engineers had to find ways to adapt an external model to the reality of Manaus. This is because, after being developed and organized at headquarters, all projects involving production and product improvement are tested in China; then, with procedural instructions, they are "sent" to the Amazon factories.

The imported technology has also required the companies' engineers to translate into Portuguese the operations that need to be implemented to make the machines work, because they are in Mandarin, the original language of instructions. An engineer from ArconChina revealed how this relationship with the headquarters occurs:

> We, from engineering in Manaus, have to contact China directly, because almost everything comes from there. That occurs because, it is China that always approves everything we do, therefore, nothing can be done without talking to China first. They want to know what is going on with us, why we have not yet introduced a certain process; so, we have to give continuous feedback to engineering there. . . . Since the factory is Chinese, they do not want Brazilian engineering to have autonomy. Therefore, we become dependent on them, because, in a crisis, it is most likely that they will fire and bring in a Chinese engineer who provides better feedback and gets paid less.
>
> *(Interview with the author, 2014)*

If on one side engineering gained prominence, despite being an imported engineering, on the other, there was a decline in the so-called "quality culture", something that was highlighted in the 1990s as a major characteristic of the Japanese production model. Workers from the surveyed factories, who pointed out how this used to be a fundamental element of the "company culture", evidenced this contrast. According to an ArconChina's machine operator:

> The Chinese want more production. They don't have that much control, and so the air conditioner can go to the customer with a leak. In the factory, the inspection is seeing something wrong, but the Chinese do not put pressure to correct it. I once worked for an American air conditioning company. Over there we were under pressure. The managers were on top of it to check on the quality issue. Here this is somewhat less so, because many defective components come from China and quality control in China and Manaus is not very strict about this.
>
> *(Interview with the author, 2014)*

The lack of the so-called "quality management" in the surveyed factories can be explained by a few reasons. First, it has to do with the general scenario that the Manaus Industrial Park has undergone in recent years. In this context, one should take into account that quality control was transferred, largely, to the very process of factory automation. In addition, the progressive increase in imported low-cost content from China and the effort to reduce expenses promoted the disarticulation of manufacturing sectors that, given a minimal production chain in Manaus, required the creation of local quality standards.

Afterward, there is a closer relationship with headquarters than with the production processes in Manaus, where almost all inputs and kits are imported. Not only that but also an expatriate management with no training in this type of quality control or, quite often, no training in engineering. The Chinese factories have furthered this trend, implementing a stricter process only when pressured by PIM customers. Finally, the local managers and engineers have little autonomy or leverage to promote quality control changes and end up assembling locally an imported engineering that, in most cases, they do not understand.

In terms of task execution, factories have given preference to workers who perform a single function, because, for the managers interviewed, they think that workers are more productive when they are specialists. However, task repetition without job rotation caused many operators to suffer repetitive strain injuries (RSI), resulting in Labor Court actions that forced factories to promote an ergonomics program and change much of the work process, by rotating the workers, performing different roles. A production leader explained how this change occurred at Motor China:

> After that, the operator is assigned to do the rotation at four jobs. So, we alternate four times by four times. The person enters, starts at the company, has a specific break of 15 minutes, which is the time to do a cycle of gymnastics, go to the bathroom, and then returns to the workstation. The company pays a professional to do 15 minutes and the employee is required to do it. When she returns from the break, she goes to another job and stays there until lunchtime. When she returns from her lunch break, she already goes to the third job. Then, there is a break in the afternoon and she proceeds to the fourth job.
>
> *(Interview with the author, 2016)*

Another Chinese characteristic in relation to global capital is that, in their search for cost reduction, some roles in the production line have been eliminated, but some that seemed to have been reduced in importance or even extinct have been reactivated. As for the first aspect, many roles have been incorporated into the factory floor operator's work, reducing salary levels and functional hierarchy. This was the case of those jobs related to final product revisions, such as the "tester" and the "calibrator", on the grounds that "the factory no longer needed them and that it would reduce unnecessary expenses by transferring these functions to production operators", as stated by a TVChina leader.

The second aspect shows the reactivation of the supervisor position, which is part of the organizational structure at TVChina, Motor China, China Board, and ArconChina. In the case of the former, there is one supervisor per production line, but if one takes into account that the coordinator also does the supervising, then direct supervision becomes a fundamental characteristic of the Chinese factories in the Manaus Industrial Park.

This type of management contrasts with the implementation of indirect factory control, a characteristic of PIM productive restructuring in the 1990s, when the "end of direct supervision" was advocated, transferring production control responsibility to the workers themselves.

Unlike this, we observe in Manaus that direct supervision is a key role played by both expatriates and local workers. That indicates a global element of the Chinese production approach since, in China itself, forms of direct control under factory supervision have also been a key part of both "disorganized despotism" and "bloody Taylorism", as shown in the studies by Lee (1999, 2007), Chan & Pun (2010), and Pun & Chan (2012).

The model of production monitoring by Chinese management has been portrayed by workers not only in terms of face-to-face, supervised control but also in terms of control through Information Technology. This monitoring is done using a system called Global System, technology that allows headquarters to visualize all worldwide production in real time and is able to direct what should be done on the factory floor.

To do so, there is an accessory system inserted into the production process where information is extracted from and passed on to the managers in China. Therefore, they know what is being produced, how many workers are working on the line, how much they are producing, and at what speed. A system analyst, responsible for the sector in the China Board company, explained how this works:

> They know when production is not meeting the requirements, then the line supervisor puts it in the system in English for everyone in China to know, what happened, why they did not produce at that specific time, etc.; and then everyone will be aware, the directors in China will know why and then complain to us.
>
> *(Interview with the author, 2016)*

At the top of this system in Manaus are Chinese managers, who set up direct connections with headquarters, creating an intense communication and work relationship between Manaus and China. This form of "transnational" control of labor is within a larger social process and is accomplished not only through information technology, via remote monitoring. It takes place under the dislocation of the Chinese labor force toward Manaus. I call this process *disciplined expatriation*, one of the forms of Chinese globalization that involves controls and disciplines.

Summary

To conclude this chapter, it is worth mentioning the basic elements that emerge from the set presented here.

First, no data was found indicating noncompliance with the Brazilian labor laws or anything of the sort, in fact, there is a Chinese tendency to adapt to the legislation, without extending beyond what is required by law. Second, Chinese capital has lower spending rates on wages and benefits when compared to other big global players in the manufacturing sector present in Manaus, especially the Japanese, South Koreans, and some Europeans. Third, there is the formation of a matrix Taylorism management, which stresses the more technical side of work under the coordination of the expatriate management.

Finally, in settings such as those of Manaus, little consideration is given to the political or diplomatic capital and to strategic interests related to the center of Chinese power, in contrast to the China–Zambia context pointed out by Lee (2017), where these elements are prized – Chinese factories have precarious labor in terms of wages, labor benefits, and worker participation. This also includes both Chinese private and state-owned enterprises, characterized as "heavy factories", with technical, bureaucratic, routine, nonparticipative management, and less flexible to changes.

In a place without major "bargaining chips" and where international companies dominate production and sales, Chinese companies follow the course, playing according to the opportunities that are posed. Among them are cost cutting and, in some respects, adopting strategies that permit them to survive or advance against competitors, such as lower cost with managers and supervisors, which is an "advantage", but makes it difficult to form production bonds with the target regions of China's advance.

Notes

1 The Brazilian Supreme Court reviewed this point by the end of 2021 and concluded that it is unconstitutional to charge the worker, even if he/she loses the lawsuit.

2 In the comparisons highlighted here, the Brazilian exchange rate was 2.35. The average minimum wage in Brazil was U$S350.00.

3 According to ILO (2016: 1), urban units "refer to state-owned urban units, urban collective ownership units, cooperative units, joint ownership units, limited liability corporations, corporations with foreign equity participation, foreign-funded units, and units with resources from Hong Kong, Macau, and Taiwan".

4 According to Moreira (2005: 27), in 2002, "wages in Brazil were three times as high as in China. In Mexico, salaries were as much as five times higher".

5 International Labour Organization. (2016), Wages, productivity and labour share in China. Research Note. April 2010. https://www.ilo.org/asia/publications/WCMS_475254/lang--en/index.htm.

6 Previously called the *multifunctional worker*. The production line worker who needs to fill any job that, for some reason, has been vacated.

5

FROM IRON RICE BOWL TO AÇAI BOWL[1]

The journey of Chinese expatriates to the Amazon

Chinese companies' internationalization and expatriation policy

Over the past few years, Chinese subsidiaries have been using expatriate labor in several countries where Chinese have made direct investments. Research such as those done by Lee (2009), Cooke (2012), and Smith & Zheng (2016) has pointed to expatriation as a "consistent mechanism" of China's foreign direct investment around the world, characterizing what may be a new wave of global labor force mobility (Smith & Zheng 2016).

For example, Lee's (2009) research on Chinese companies in Zambia and Tanzania revealed expatriation as a tool used by Chinese transnationals to maintain control of operations abroad and to operationalize a certain type of labor relationship based on subcontracting, temporary work, loss of rights and benefits, low wages – local workers refer as "slave wages" (Lee 2009: 651) – and the use of long working hours. The author categorized this process as a *casualization in Africa's Chinese enclaves*. One of the factories investigated by Lee (2009) had almost 200 Chinese nationals occupying the most important managerial and technical positions.

Other parts of the globe have also experienced processes similar to those observed by Lee (2009) on the African continent. As an example, Cooke (2012) found that in Huawei's subsidiaries in India, Chinese expatriates accounted for nearly 30% of the company's workforce, with more revenue generated abroad than in China itself.

In the European case, the research by Smith & Zheng (2016) showed that at a Huawei subsidiary in Istanbul, Turkey, from a total of 1,000 employees, about 200 of them were Chinese (one in five). For the authors, this high rate of expatriates seems to be unique.

DOI: 10.4324/9781003229377-5

Chinese expatriate mobility and its distribution at all levels of subsidiaries is a key feature of Chinese global expansion and a reflection of two movements: First, the availability of low-cost, trained workers in the country fit to work abroad. Second, as a new player in global capitalism, Chinese companies seek to deploy an international-sized workforce while maintaining coercive controls on the freedom of Chinese workers abroad (Smith & Zheng 2016).

Furthermore, the authors point out that

> Expats are there (abroad) because they follow Chinese firm tenets, they are more focused on work, and, as migrants usually live in company-based industrial dormitories, they are tightly controlled and more likely to focus on work during the contract period and submit to compulsory overtime, which is resisted by local workers, and work flexibly with less voice, which locals shun. . . . Here, it is not the nationality of labor, which is important, but rather the level of dependency of workers in the overseas location.
>
> *(Smith & Zheng 2016: 376)*

For Lee (2009), this element of Chinese workers' expatriation to other productive territories emerges as a way to create "enclaves" ("flying lands", in Chinese translation). A unique territorial, cultural, and social unit, enclosed within the foreign territory, because, according to the author, the Chinese expatriates have a form of sociability and factory practices that seek to reproduce work systems from China's perspective. Notwithstanding this, workers' pressures and movements end up with negotiations between expatriate and the "native", as observed by Lee (2009) in Zambia and Tanzania, creating tensions in "expatriate enclaves", which may become more or less integrated into the local manufacturing context.

In a recent survey in Zambia, Lee (2017) shows that expatriates comprised 5% to 10% of the workforce. Compared to other foreign private investments, whose expatriation focus is on managers' individual careers, Chinese state capital bases expatriation on a collective project and has at its disposal an arguably more controlled, disciplined, and frugal managerial workforce. This is also reinforced by the government discourse of China's victimization by the West, causing expatriates to have "Eating Bitterness" – which are moral and nationalistic boundaries that cover up the class exploitation inflicted by Chinese investment.

The disciplined expatriation policy in Manaus

In the case of the Amazon, one of the first aspects that drew attention in the Chinese factories located in Manaus was the number of expatriates. The number of expatriates within the organizational structure in the surveyed companies was distributed as follows: 10 at MotorChina, 20 at China Board, 30 at ArconChina, and 50 at TVChina, which represents almost 10% of the total workforce, while the percentage of expatriates in other foreign companies represented no more than 1%.

TABLE 5.1 – Profile of interviewed Chinese expatriates (2016)

Interviewee	*Sex*	*Age*	*Schooling*	*Time in the company**	*Post*
1. Henrique Wang	M	33	College degree	Not informed	Production manager
2. Roger Nang	M	32	College degree	16 years	Process engineering manager
3. Liu Feng	M	30	College degree	12 years	Quality manager
4. Marcos Lee	M	35	College degree	11 years	Materials/supplies manager
5. André Shang	M	34	College degree	10 years	Import manager
6. Liz Yang	F	41	College degree	Not informed	Industrial director
7. Wenguan Deng	M	Not informed	College degree	Not informed	Industrial director
8. Hao Zhung	M	28	College degree	Not informed	Production supervisor
9. Anne Ching	F	32	College degree	10 years	Engineering manager

Source: Data collected and compiled by the author.

* Adding both Brazil and China.

In order to understand how the expatriation process works and how the Chinese are inserted into the manufacturing environment in Manaus, I conducted interviews with nine of them. Table 5.1 shows the main information on the profile of these interviewees.

According to the local manager responsible for China Board's Chinese expatriation, an expatriation occurs when the local company has a "need". He addressed this issue in the following words:

> When there is a need, we have a position but we probably don't have people specialized for the activity here in Manaus. So, we have in China a variety of highly qualified people with few job opportunities. Moreover, since we are a Chinese company here, if opportunity X arises, we send the position opening to China.
>
> *(Interview with the author, 2015)*

A different view was presented by a TVChina manager, who does not consider a matter of looking abroad for a type of worker inexistent in Brazil:

> The truth is that the Chinese prefer to give opportunities for professional growth to other Chinese. There is an expatriate who came here as a production line repair technician and now he works as a manager. Of course, there were people in Manaus who were qualified for this. . . . We have people

> from Brazil qualified for the position, but because the Chinese already works for the company in China, they move them to another country. . . . They work very hard, and the opportunities in China are very limited. So, when an opportunity arises here, they are already in line, because the salary here is twice as high as those paid there, and there is a growth in the hierarchy, which is very important for them.
>
> *(Interview with the author, 2015)*

For ArconChina's HR manager, the presence of Chinese in Manaus is due to a communication difficulty between China and Brazil:

> There are Chinese at all levels of the organization; you just don't have them at the operational assembly level. However, engineering, controller assistants, quality assistance, you have it all. Then, it also extends to the supervisory, coordinating, and managerial levels. They intermingle in such a way to permit them to observe the whole company; and I understood that this is also a Chinese culture to facilitate their communication. . . . Because even in European countries where English is not the native language there are many citizens who master this language, making it easier to communicate with other people. In China, one can see that English proficiency is scarcer. Thus, the presence of expatriates helps to break the language barriers.
>
> *(Interview with the author, 2014)*

According to MotorChina Company's industrial director, it is a "cultural issue": "The Chinese don't relinquish the idea of having Chinese managers at all hierarchical levels of the company. This is typical of their management". According to the evaluation given by a quality manager, "there is no need for so many Chinese here in Manaus. We have people who question this process. Since the company is Chinese, this is beyond our control, that is, to say whether the factory should be this way or not".

The recruitment of expatriates is done in China, where a group of workers is evaluated, and their professional profiles are sent to the subsidiary manager in Manaus. The manager interviews the candidates, conducts tests on the production process via Skype, and then sends the results to the head office, which decides which worker will be expatriated.

When there is a job opening in Manaus, the competition for this is almost 500 people. The enticements include a salary higher than that earned in China, the money sent to families living in the countryside, and the possibility to expand one's resume. There is also a housing allowance in Manaus and trips to China once a year, which usually take place around February, the Chinese New Year.

As to the recruitment procedure, it is worth mentioning that, at the very beginning of the expatriations, the local interviews were conducted by Brazilian managers. However, as the Chinese workers arrived and took over the most qualified positions in Manaus, the selection process began to be carried out by the Chinese, which denotes a change in the expatriation policy operationalization, transferred from Brazilians in Manaus to the head office in China.

In general, the work contract for an opening in Manaus is for a period of two years, but some distinguished workers have their contracts renewed. A manager responsible for the expatriations explained how this displacement process happens:

> The work visa granted to them in China is for two years. This work visa can be extended for another two years. Now, a new law is in effect whereby he/she can transform this temporary stay directly into a permanent one, with a ten-year duration. The reason for this is to avoid the red tape required by the Federal Police, the Ministry of Justice, and the Ministry of Labor. It makes things easier for expatriates, even though most of them come with a two-year work visa, then, if necessary, we extend it for two more years and so on.
>
> *(Interview with the author, 2015)*

The field research showed two types of expatriates: those who go to Manaus for a specific purpose – to solve an ongoing company problem, to teach how to assemble a new product, and to supervise the workforce – and those previously assigned to manage the factory, as reported by a quality manager:

> Every Chinese individual who comes to Brazil has a key objective to fulfill and focuses on this. They work harder than most Brazilians. They come to improve a process that is not working well. Therefore, whoever comes from China is anything but an operator, even a repair technician comes. They have a mission.
>
> *(Interview with the author, 2016)*

When compared to Brazilian managers, the expatriates are mostly young, even the managers, whose average age is around 30, while the Brazilian managers are, on average, around 36. According to the expatriates' view, the worker has to become a supervisor by the time he/she is 20. Up to 25, you have to be a coordinator, and by the time you are 30, a manager, "otherwise you can't do it anymore, because in China the competition is intense".

For Brazilian workers who deal directly with the Chinese, expatriates have a rigid relation with the hierarchical issue: they establish no intimacy with the factory floor workers, they continue to serve their superiors even outside the factory and do not mind earning less than their Brazilian subordinates, as they are specialists:

> Here they earn three times more than in China. However, compared to Brazilians, they earn less. For example: as an area coordinator, I earned more than my Chinese boss did. In the Chinese environment, any specialist earns more than their boss does. This does not happen in the Brazilian model.
>
> *(Interview with the author, 2014)*

Such view was also shared by a China Board engineering analyst: "I earn more than my Chinese boss, but they don't mind that. In Brazil, it is different. If you are a boss, you earn more than your subordinate". Again, by an HR manager, "They consider the hierarchical position better than the salary. The Brazilian wants the bonus in cash. The Chinese, on the other hand, if you say, 'you went from level four to level five', they become much happier".

These interviewees' comments revealed, among other things, what we can call the "cultural characteristics of expatriation", where its hierarchical aspect emerges as one of the basic components of both social relations among expatriates and business relations. This hierarchy is based on Guanxi – whose main bases for relationships are loyalty, moral leadership, the flow of trust, the spirit of harmony, hierarchy among different people, and the obligation of bonds – as well as on the nationalist idea of overcoming poverty and China's expansion around the world.

This process places the expatriates as external agents of Chinese globalization, being morally and even subjectively required to engage with a subordinated and disciplined behavior toward headquarters. In practical terms, this makes up the modern influence of Chinese culture on its internal and external managerial processes and is in line with the observations made by Chen & Lee (2008), Pinheiro-Machado (2011), and Lee (2017), which shows the power of cultural elements in China's social relations. Therefore, Guanxi and nationalism are intertwined in the Chinese model and reflect on how it manages its factories globally, as a *culturally disciplined expatriation*.

Moreover, it is a product of expatriation "material" aspect based on a Chinese worker's relation to socioeconomic needs, which subordinates himself to the hierarchies to obtain higher earnings for himself and his family in China, therefore, configuring a *materially disciplined expatriation*. Thus, *Guanxi* and nationalism are a kind of "spirit" of Chinese expatriation, to use an expression coined by Max Weber. This cultural dimension of expatriation creates the "spiritual" conditions for the Chinese material subordination abroad.

Another point mentioned by the managers of the local factories about the Chinese expatriates, concerns a certain difficulty that these ones have to understand the Brazilian labor legislation:

> They don't have much respect for local labor. When you talk to Chinese managers, you notice that they are amazed at the amount of labor laws. They think it is an exaggeration. If you tell them that you are not allowed to work more than 10 hours a day, they don't believe you. If a machine breaks down, the Chinese want me to call the employee on vacation to fix the machines, but I tell them that they cannot. However, they have an almost religious discipline for compliance with the law. Therefore, even though, they are appalled by the CLT, if they know that it is the law, they will comply. When I want to get something for the sector, I get to the Chinese showing them that it is the law, and they immediately do it.
>
> *(Interview with the author, 2014)*

In conversations with the Chinese workers, they were rather reticent about the subject, avoiding talking about it whenever I tried to introduce them to this type of issue. Nevertheless, after establishing greater proximity, they expressed their ideas about work in Brazil, indicating that the local worker is "very privileged, protected, and not very productive", as said to me by this expatriate:

> Here the labor union protects the worker too much. In China it is different. For example, if a person does something wrong there, it is easy to fire him. Here, they would consider this as an irregularity. In China they are not so protective. I think that work here is better. I mean, it is better for the worker, because for the company it is not as good. There are many costs involved with the Brazilian worker.
>
> *(Interview with the author, 2015)*

It is important to point out that *disciplined expatriation* also becomes a form of disciplining the local labor force. The expatriate needs to provide daily feedback to the Chinese headquarters, through reports and conversations using digital media about the daily production, the major problems found in the company, how the local worker is behaving, why the company's goals were not met, and things that result in a burden being placed on the Manaus worker.

In the case of Brazilian supervisors, these demands are expressed through weekly reports sent in English, detailing their weekly production. For shop floor leaders, the demand is daily, because they need to feed, every half hour, the system that shows the local production in Manaus.

Its implications for the workers result from a chain of events: the leaders feed the system; the system informs the Chinese from headquarters; these ones question the Chinese expatriates at the subsidiary, who question factory floor leaders, who question operators. One worker reported, "the Chinese monitor us on a big screen to see if we are meeting our production goals. If not, they do not stop making demands on production. They demand a lot! They are always on the production line supervising us".

An engineering technician also described this process, showing that Chinese's demands are high:

> Once a week I write a report describing what I did wrong, what I did to fix it, and what I will do next time. Then I send it to China. The person responsible for giving the feedback is a Brazilian manager. They are bureaucratic, they like reports. These reports give me a lot of work. At the end of the shift, I spend about twenty minutes and filling out a spreadsheet that describes what happens on the job. Besides that daily report, there is the weekly report. This is the "Chinese culture".
>
> *(Interview with the author, 2016)*

In addition to pressuring both upper hierarchical level workers and those on the factory floor, the disciplined expatriation creates a conflict between Brazilians and

Chinese expatriates. This happens because, according to HR managers, during periods of crisis, it is more difficult to fire a Chinese worker, because the Chinese head office "protects" the employee, therefore, it is the Brazilian employee who ends up being fired.

Therefore, in 2015, during a "lunch conversation" with TVChina's Human Resources manager, he informed me that he had to lay off some workers due to low demand for TVs, but that it was difficult to lay off the Chinese, because they had the "protection from head office" that would not allow them to be fired "at all".

During an interview with a female employee, she reported the following:

> During economic crises, the Brazilians are the ones most likely to leave because there will always be favoritism. Despite the fact that they try to oppose it, favoritism is always going to exist. As a result, the Chinese always win and the Brazilians are at the mercy of it, in a secondary level.
>
> *(Interview with the author, 2014)*

In addition to these aspects, expatriation also functions as a cost reduction mechanism and an advantage for the Chinese industry. This happens because in general the surveyed factories pay the expatriate a salary lower than that paid to a Brazilian for the same job. Tables 5.2 and 5.3 illustrate this statement.[2] In the first, a

TABLE 5.2 – Comparison of salaries between headquarters and subsidiaries – ArconChina

Average wage at ArconChina (US$)			
Post	*Wage of Brazilians*	*Wage of expatriates*	*Wage in China*
Director	Not informed	Not informed	Not informed
Manager	2340.00	1690.00	1380.00
Coordinator	2130.00	1480.00	1000.00
Supervisor	1700.00	1200.00	980.00
Operator	570.00	No expatriates	750.00

Source: Statistics collected and compiled by the author.

Note: Company names are fictitious.

TABLE 5.3 – Comparison of salaries between headquarters and subsidiaries – TVChina

Average wage at TVChina (US$)			
Post	*Wage of Brazilians*	*Wage of expatriates*	*Wage in China*
Director	14000.00	12700.00	Not informed
Manager	8500.00	7000.00	3900.00
Coordinator	4900.00	4200.00	2050.00
Supervisor	3180.00	2500.00	1380.00
Operator	480.00	No expatriates	590.00

Source: Statistics collected and compiled by the author.

Note: Company names are fictitious.

comparison is made between the salaries of Brazilians and expatriates who occupy the same post at ArconChina in Manaus and how much a Chinese worker earns in the same post at the headquarters in China. The other table makes a same type of comparison at TVChina.

Despite the fact that the salaries of operational workers are higher at headquarters than in the subsidiaries, it is important to point out that the salaries of the highest hierarchical level in Manaus are more than double those paid in China, a difference that increases according to the hierarchical position. This is in line with Arrighi's (2007: 366), who reports that

> Indeed, for the most part, the main competitive advantage of China is not that its production workers typically cost 5 percent of their US counterparts but that its engineers and plant managers cost 35 percent or less. . . . Chinese businesses substitute inexpensive educated labor, not just for expensive machinery, but for expensive managers as well.

PIM's Chinese expatriates' payment is made in local currency, and a good part of the amounts are usually transferred by expatriates whose families stayed in China. When the exchange rate is favorable to the expatriate, they transfer almost all of their salary. If not, they retain it and wait for the scenario to change. In some companies, there was a bank branch within the factory site specialized in making bank transfers to the families of the Chinese employees.

As highlighted earlier, the Chinese expatriates' salaries are associated with the concession of some benefits, such as apartments and an annual air ticket to China, indicating some form of salary equivalence when compared to Brazil. However, the fact is that these benefits are granted in the form of rented apartments – as a kind of *controlled dormitory*[3] – shared by as many as five expatriates, which considerably reduces the costs for the subsidiary companies and does not equalize the salaries of expatriates with those of the Brazilians.

Moreover, although the "red envelope" (紅包, hóngbāo) is something common at the beginning of every New Year in China, as a "bonus" for the workers, this is not done in Manaus. According to information provided by the expatriates, such a bonus is not given to local managers and workers, and neither between the Chinese head office and the expatriates, it is a practice restricted to Mainland China.

The expatriation from below

Apart from trying to understand the Chinese production model through the logic of capital and its formal channels, I also intended to understand it as human activity and agency in the new global economy spearheaded by China. The expatriates formed a fundamental part of this. Therefore, it was necessary to learn who they were, give them faces, identify the social and subjective reasons for their actions, and the contexts that converged to enable this new labor route between China and the Amazon. Therefore, it was necessary to proceed with the analysis of an "expatriation from below", in order to observe Chinese globalization in its weaknesses, contexts, instabilities, and insecurities.

From this perspective of analysis, I will present this China/Manaus route through three Chinese expatriates with whom I was in contact during the years I was conducting the field research. As a fundamental element of this process, there is the fact of their birth in a China that was undergoing economic and social reforms and, eventually, entering the globalized world. There are also the difficulties faced in the Chinese rural environment, their access to the country's universities, the logic of migration from rural to urban areas, the insertion mode in the headquarters' manufacturing universe, and the reasons behind the transfers to the subsidiaries in Manaus, and their plans.

In order to comprehend this social entanglement from an angle that relates biography, geography, nation, and history, I use the idea of "journey". As pointed out by Knowles (2014), this is a "middle range" category aimed to analyze globalization through human agency and their mobility within translocally connected social "trails". Therefore, journeys, are a kind of map of people and the places they travel through, to permit a way of thinking about them, incorporating space and movement.

In the idea of *journey*, the central issue consists in understanding the "spatial biography" of individuals, which allows us to interpret globalization from its "secondary roads". This means investigating it beyond its main roads, which is where almost everything we know about globalization is derived from (Knowles 2014).

However, by focusing on the trails, the "alternative" paths, we gain human agency and reveal important aspects of globalization, such as global migration, exposing processes that go beyond transference of manufacturing plants, state-of-the-art technology and machinery, information, capital flows, and product chains, leading us to a new feature of Chinese expansion: the expatriate and their journeys.

André Shang's journey

The first contact with an expatriate was with André Shang,[4] 32 years old, an ArconChina import manager, responsible for purchasing products from the Chinese headquarters to Brazil. He had been in Brazil for six years, married, but his wife and son stayed in China after spending three months in Manaus and not adapting to the city, and because the cost of living was higher.

Referred to me by a ZFM civil servant, who gave me Shang's phone number, I met with him three times between 2014 and 2016. Our first contact was in 2014 during a scheduled visit to the ArconChina factory. He was the one who received my research assistant and me and showed us the company's manufacturing processes. In 2015, I returned to the city of Manaus for field research and contacted Shang to arrange another conversation, this time outside the factory.

Since he had already declined other contact attempts, I was quite afraid that nothing would work out or that he would not give me any in-depth information. Nevertheless, we met on a weekend, at lunchtime, which he considered more convenient, in a shopping mall near his workplace. The beginning of our conversation consisted of short answers, in English, without venturing into any of the topics I was aiming at, only about basic company data. My strategy was to wait for "the best moment" to talk about something more related to my research objective, especially about the managerial aspect.

Unaware of the exact moment, I asked Shang if he wanted something to eat and, seizing the opportunity, I tried to introduce management topics, expatriation issues, and characteristics of air-conditioning production. Not waiting for our drinks to arrive, Shang said he could not talk about any of those subjects, left the table, and suddenly left the mall telling me:

> Friend, I wanted to help you. But, I don't want any complications for me, okay? Now, I have to leave. Bye.
>
> *(Interview with the author, 2014)*

Despite Shang's denial and the apparent failure of this interview, a few days later I contacted him again and thanked him for his kindness in receiving me at the factory and later at the mall. After returning to the state of São Paulo, where I was working on my PhD in Sociology, and reporting these events to my advisor and our research group, I would occasionally send a cell phone message asking Shang about how he was doing, if he had visited China, etc. Most of the time he did not answer, and sometimes he would just say "I am in China", "I am in the factory now", and "I am fine".

During a field trip to Manaus at the beginning of 2015, I informed him that I was in the city and if I could talk to him again. To my surprise and joy, Shang said yes, already specifying the location – the same mall as in 2014 – the day, and time of the conversation, only recommending me not to put his real name in my research and that I should not extend the interview time too much, because other expats "would need to use the company car" as well.

This time, information began to emerge and Shang told me about other subjects of a more personal nature, something that occurred again in 2016, during another field visit, always at the same shopping mall in Manaus. In addition to these meetings, I also kept in touch with him through text messages over the years. But most of the information gathered was in person, with dynamics typical of a sociological investigation that sometimes reaches the limits of despair feeling that everything is lost and other times emerges as unexpected answers that renew the researcher's expectations.

It was within this context of despair and unplanned outings that I received information about expatriation as well as André Shang's own life as a *journey*.

Like many of China's post-opening youth, Shang was born in a small village in Hunan Province, the birthplace of Communist leader Mao Zedong. Shang's family consisted of very poor farming parents, who grew rice and vegetables and taught him to do the farm's heavy lifting. The entire production was family-owned and aimed to be consumed by its members, as he told me:

> We planted only for our own food. We didn't sell anything. My parents wanted me to study and go to university and work in a big city. However, they had no idea of a profession for me, neither many resources. They just thought I should go to a good university.
>
> *(Interview with the author, 2015)*

When Shang finished his village education at the age of 17, he went to study at a university in another Chinese province, which he said was made possible by the *hukou* system of university migration, which allowed students to transfer their system of residence to their place of study. Something unlikely for the Mao era peasant generation, such as that of Shang's parents who, due to hard work in the rural areas, could not complete their studies. The post-economic opening generation has had greater access to education, being able to attend college and even migrate to other places in China.

Shang majored in Materials Engineering during a four-year period in a public university, paying a small fee per year. During this period, his parents sent him a monthly stipend to support his studies, something made possible by an increase in harvests, the modernization of China's agriculture, and the possibility of selling their produce to the market. As a result, they managed to save some money and pay for the university fees where Shang studied.

ArconChina hired Shang when he was in his last year of college, at the age of 22. It was his first job.

> I graduated from university in 2004. In China it is like this: many companies go to universities to hire graduates. These universities choose the people to go straight to the company. They don't choose only the best students. It depends on the need. If you study Arts it is more difficult. It depends on the area you study.
>
> *(Interview with the author, 2015)*

Shang spent two years as a junior process engineer, learning to deal with the entire component manufacturing system of the company. André Shang lived in a dormitory in Zhuhai, a city in Guangdong Province where the head office is located in China, along with other workers, a very common practice in China, especially for migrant workers, such as this expatriate. In a demonstration of how language difficulties can be a problem during sociological interviews, I asked Shang, in Portuguese, if the company dormitory was inside the factory, meaning located inside the company compound. But the word "inside" visibly upsets him a lot. The following dialog exposes this "critical moment" of the field research on the day we met in a shopping mall in Manaus, when I thought that this contact would be terminated (the sentences in parentheses correspond to my questions):

> (Did you live in a company dormitory in Zhuhai?) Company dormitory. But, I paid a symbolic price. (Was the dormitory inside the factory?) No, the

> factory is just a factory. Nobody makes a dormitory inside the factory. I am saying that ArconChina offered a dormitory for its employees. As it does here, but not inside the factory. A factory is a factory, do you know? (I have read research that says that many factories in China have dormitories . . .). This is crazy! I think it is crazy! A factory is a factory! Within a factory you can't have a dormitory, you can't smoke, to avoid catching fire. That's crazy. (See, Shang, I don't think "inside" is the right word, I don't mean that. Maybe the more appropriate word is "near" the factory). Humm . . . there is a dormitory nearby. (So, in China is the proximity like your apartment here in Manaus?) In China, the dormitory is even closer to the factory. It is in the same city. The distance in China is like this: here is the dormitory. Cross the street and you have the factory. It is two minutes away. It is close.
>
> *(Interview with the author, 2015)*

After the conversation between Shang and me reached an "understanding", he proceeded to tell me about his expatriation to Manaus occurred:

> It was in 2007. ArconChina needed people, and the director in Brazil requested the headquarters in China for employees interested in going to Brazil. Interested employees should send their resume to ArconChina's HR in China. I left my resume. I was very young, and I wanted to have experience so, I thought that Brazil would be fundamental. I saw coming to Brazil as an opportunity to get to know another country. I had never left China before.
>
> *(Interview with the author, 2015)*

Driven by the desire to gain experience and thereby increase his chances of growth in the company, Shang reported that he decided to take the risk, even though there was only one vacancy available for 49 candidates,[5] and he was the one selected during the selection process. In his opinion, the company took into account his fluency in English and the experience he had with air-conditioning assembly.

> Speaking English helped a lot, but so did my experience in the air-conditioning assembly process. They saw that, since I was qualified in this area, I would be able to import inputs correctly. In addition, I told the director in Brazil that I really wanted to get to know another country. When I was approved, my parents were very happy, because they put me first in their lives. I was not married at the time, nor did I have a girlfriend. Now, the part about getting the documentation to come to Brazil was very difficult. It took about 6 months from the day I was chosen until I received my visa.
>
> *(Interview with the author, 2015)*

The remark made by Shang – that one of the main reasons why he was hired was his ability to correctly import inputs – confirms the way the Chinese company is operationalized in Manaus, where importing is a primary input acquisition tool, as we saw in Chapter 3. An example, Shang stated – like the other interviewees – that the increase in the exchange rate, intensified by the financial crisis in Brazil, since 2015, was very bad for business, because it made inputs more expensive and affected the factory's productivity. On this issue, he pointed out that

> Now everything is normal, but then again we are not growing much. Our goal last year (2014) was to increase production this year (2015). However, due to the high exchange rate, we just can't do that. Here in Manaus we had as many as 350 employees in 2013, but after production dropped, we had to lay off some people, and now we are maintaining the same amount of employees since 2014, which is 300 people.
>
> *(Interview with the author, 2015)*

Despite all the difficulties faced by the company in terms of production expansion caused by the economic crisis that resulted in a decrease in import capacity and sales, and the fall in the consumers' purchasing power, Shang pointed out possibilities for long-term change in this scenario. He stated that being in Brazil is very positive because of their access to the same labor rights assured to other Brazilian employees:

> Here in Brazil, my vacations are paid by the company, including the plane tickets to China. The company also pays for my apartment, including the water bill. I only pay the electricity bill. I also have health insurance, food baskets, and other benefits offered to Brazilians. This is good, different from my work in China.
>
> *(Interview with the author, 2016)*

In addition, as a manager, Shang made twice as much as his salary in China and was responsible for interviewing candidates for management positions coming from China to ArconChina in Manaus. He returned to China every six months to visit his parents, wife, and son. He told me that he had thought of living in Brazil, but his wife, when she visited him, did not adapt to the city of Manaus:

> I might will go back to China at the end of the year (2016). In the second semester, my son will go to school. He is five years old. He already understands many things and asks me to go back, to stay with them in China. However, actually, I wanted to live in Brazil, if I was not married. However, when you are married, there is a problem, because my wife[6] and son don't want to live here. If they wanted to live here with me, I would have no problem staying longer in Brazil.
>
> *(Interview with the author, 2016)*

Just like the other interviewees, Shang remitted part of his salary to his family in China, because, according to him, the living conditions there are more difficult and his wife and son depend on his work in Brazil. These are all the reasons why he has stayed so long in Manaus. However, he says that going back to China is always on his mind because he misses his family.

As far as how his feedback with the Chinese headquarters occurs, he stated they communicate mainly through e-mail. However, as he became more comfortable with the conversation, he reported that he has to be at the headquarters available almost every day during the nights to deal with issues concerning production in Manaus:

> If it is something of great importance and urgency, when I come home from work, I talk to the head office. Because, although it is night here, it is day in China. Therefore, when Brazilians leave work, they have nothing else to do, but, in our case, it is different. We have to talk to China almost on a daily basis. I have to check with them if everything is ready, if the ship has left and, when new products are launched and they want to send them to us, I have to talk to them about PPB, because they don't know the laws here in Manaus. I cannot communicate well by E-mail; I prefer to explain these things using the Internet or telephone. In China, I talk to the export support sector. This is the sector I talk to.
>
> *(Interview with the author, 2016)*

This control of the headquarters with the expatriate workers – also observed in other interviewees' comments – is a factor that makes work tiring and exhausting, because, in some cases, according to Shang, the conversations can last until the early hours of the morning, even though they have to be back at work early the next day.

Roger Nang's journey

The second interview was conducted with Roger Nang, 32 years old, a process engineering manager at TVChina. Nang was born in a small village in the Fujian Province and has lived in Manaus for nine years. In 2014, when I first interviewed him, Nang was living alone in Manaus, because his wife and son had stayed in China. In early 2015, the time of the second interview, his wife and son had come to live with him, but they did not adapt and returned to China after four months.

Of all the interviewees, Nang was the one I had more contact with and also the one who gave me access to other interviewees, such as Marcos Lee, whose journey will be addressed later. My first conversation with him took place at TVChina, through a referral from the company's Human Resources manager, who gathered several expatriates in a factory room and allowed us to talk to them at the beginning of 2014. As previously indicated in the introduction to this volume, these formal interviews were important for a first contact with the Chinese, but they provided little information on their lives and trajectories. Therefore, as soon as the interview was finished, my assistant and I asked for the phone numbers of two expatriates who had stayed until the end of the interview: Roger Nang and his Chinese colleague, Anne Ching, an engineering manager.

A few days later, I contacted Anne Ching, asking if we could meet for a meal and a chat. She replied that she liked the idea and that she would invite another Chinese friend of hers to come with us. To our surprise, it was Roger Nang, one of the interviewees at the factory.

We had been informed that the expatriates liked to eat Brazilian beef, therefore, we took them to a shopping mall where a famous Manaus steakhouse was located. However, they were the ones who determined the final destination of the meeting: they picked us up at the mall and took us for soup at another restaurant, with Nang justifying the change of route in these terms:

> Today we will have soup, then, in the next interview, you will take us to eat meat, ok? Soup is a very popular dish in China, but little appreciated in Brazil. Here people like fatty foods, meat, salt, sugar and fried food. I am even surprised that you are thin, because you tend to be fatter here in Manaus.
>
> *(Interview with the author, 2014)*

When we got there, the first thing that caught our attention was that Anne Ching held my assistant's arms and stayed like that all the way to the soup house. It looked as if they were already great friends, something that encouraged us greatly, because, in our minds, arms given would mean a greater possibility of access to information and data.

Thus, in planning our interviews, I was almost certain that the most important information about expatriation would come from Anne Ching, because she was open from the beginning of our contacts and even afterward, taking us to her home, preparing Chinese meals for us, and always trying to find out a little about our lives in Brazil. However, despite her great kindness and friendliness, she hardly let us into subjects that involved anything beyond the "technicalities" of her work at TVChina. Moreover, during conversations attended by other Chinese nationals, the male expatriates dominated the topics discussed, leaving little room for Ching to express herself.

The fact is that, after two years of these first contacts, she returned to China and we no longer had any form of communication. Nevertheless, Anne Ching was fundamental to our research: she opened doors in the company, guided us during our visit to the TV manufacturing sector, introduced us to other Chinese people, and took us to see where they lived and what the expatriate apartments were like. She always welcomed us with great and fun conversations about various Amazon topics although little about the expatriate system itself.

During my first contact at the soup restaurant, they were very happy to establish bonds with people associated with the university and to be able to escape from the work routine. As a result, talking about this topic did not raise any interest in them, at least at that moment, and, later on, I understood this, at that level of friendship. While work for Brazilians is the subject of a conversation circle, of public space, for Chinese expatriates work is a sphere very much related to their intimacy, only accessed after some Guanxi has been established.

Therefore, the big topic of conversation was their impressions and questions about Brazil, especially about government and economic trends and about my and my research assistant's plans. This gave us the opportunity to learn about their projects while in Brazil.

Roger Nang told us that he wanted to be an entrepreneur in Amazonas, taking goods from China to the city of Manaus and vice versa, because, according to him, he wanted to have more financial autonomy. Anne Ching, on the other hand, said she wanted to study for an MBA, but that she had not yet done due to her difficulty with the Portuguese language.

When dinner was over, and it was time to leave, Roger Nang got up from the table and insisted on paying the bill, because in his view we were his guests. He also said that he would drive us home, and so it happened. On the way to our residence in Manaus, we agreed to go to my mother's farm in rural Amazonas and they liked the idea.

Two weeks later, Nang, Ching and another expatriate picked us up at home and we went to the farm, under my promise of a big *tambaqui* fishing trip. The idea was to create bonds, to show that we were opening our lives to them. Despite the promise of the researcher, we arrived under heavy rain in the rural area and caught nothing but a few *tambaqui* from a pond owned by a friend, a fish farmer in the region. However, bonds were being formed and, little by little, information about their lives and about the meaning of expatriation began to emerge.

Every time I returned to Manaus, in 2015, 2016, and 2017, I went out with Nang. Sometimes Ching would go with him, before she went back to China. In 2015, Marcos Lee and another Chinese also visited my house in Manaus. After the field research, even though I was in another state, I kept talking to him by messaging app. In 2018, after I finished my research, I returned to Manaus, and this time Nang's wife and son were on vacation, visiting him. It was the first time I saw her, but we hardly talked, because she spoke neither English nor Portuguese and, besides, she had just arrived from China and was visibly tired and adapting to the Brazilian time zone.

This close relationship with Nang made it possible to obtain a lot of information not only about the television manufacturing process but about his own life and work trajectory, on how he became an expatriate.

One of many interviews with Nang was in a public house in a Manaus shopping mall. He had just returned from a vacation in China, and complained of sore throats caused by the air pollution in his country, and he told us that his wife had come to spend a few days with him.

> So far, it has been good for her (the wife). Because she has her husband here. The air is good here, because the air in China is not good to breathe. I was not feeling well breathing the air in China. The air is dirty, there. There is much more dust on it. However, it was very good for me (referring to the

> vacation in China). I saw my family. I brought them here for a few days. Now my work is very intense. Sometimes I don't have time to take care of my family. TVChina is a very demanding company, we are very busy. There is a lot of work. Zheng (his boss) told me: "You need to come back to Brazil ready to solve problems, because we need to implement automotive projects". Then I only had 30 days of vacation this time. Other people take 45-day vacation.
>
> *(Interview with the author, 2015)*

Nang grew up in a rural area of southeastern China. His father grew rice, tea, and peaches, and he helped grow these crops, along with his sisters. But, when he turned 17, his parents wanted Nang to go to college. However, they did not have the money to send him to the university, because an adverse weather condition in 1998 made the family lose all their agricultural production. The solution was to borrow money from relatives so that they could send their son to continue his studies. When Nang entered college, his family was able to move to the city to make it easier for their only male child to attend university. This shift in location led his father to become a small businessperson,[7] and to give up farming.

In the city, Nang went to college to study agronomy. According to Nang, "without having much idea what it was", when he graduated, a college friend who worked at the TVChina called to say that the factory's production was high and they were hiring workers. He went for an interview at the company's HR department and got the job as a production operator.

> When I was working as an operator at TVChina, I saw people fixing TV monitors and I thought it was cool. Then I went to talk to one of these people: "What you are doing is interesting". Then, I realized that the person was very focused on doing that. I found out that the salary of the person who fixed the monitor was higher than mine, so I began to study. When my shift was over I would not leave the factory. I stayed for the second shift, to learn by watching the guy fix it. I helped him fix the machine, as a result, he started to teach me. When I moved to the second shift at the company, I would come into the factory two or three hours earlier to learn. Then people started to notice me as someone interested and said: "his guy really wants to learn". So everyone taught me and I started to learn a little more about electronic processes on my own.
>
> *(Interview with the author, 2015)*

Nang reported that he worked so hard on his job that he worked extra hours in order to get a promotion and a better salary in the crowded and competitive Chinese labor market. As a result, with many more hours of work and no overtime pay, he got a position as an electronics technician and eventually became a leader. It was within this context of greater prominence in the company that Nang was informed, in 2005, about the opening of a position of electronic process supervisor at the TVChina factory in Manaus. He applied for the job along with 20 other candidates. He says that the fact that he knew English and had shown interest when he worked on the factory floor in China helped him a lot during the selection process.

Nang also mentioned that he was very excited when the opportunity for the job in Manaus came up, because, according to him,

> There is a lot of competition in China. There are many people wanting to work, and there are not many benefits as there are here. In addition, traveling to another country is very important in China, because people are curious to know the experience of those who work abroad.
>
> *(Interview with the author, 2016)*

The symbolic value of traveling abroad, highlighted by Nang, is in line with the observation of Pinheiro-Machado (2011) in relation to Chinese culture, that is, that these symbolisms are structuring social and economic relations in China. In the case of expatriation, becoming an expatriate worker causes the individual's Guanxi to expand, granting him a greater possibility not only of permanence but also of ascension and social mobility in the Chinese labor market. Furthermore, there is pride within the family and among the expatriate's neighbors, as Nang pointed out, "Everyone in my village and in my family was happy that I got the job".

Since his transfer to Manaus, Nang has held the position of supervisor and coordinator. When the field research was done, he was the manager of electronic process engineering and earned almost twice as much as what he would receive in China, despite the fact that his salary was around half of what a Brazilian manager would receive for the same position.

Even though he is in Manaus in a higher position than the one he held in China, he pointed out that he still behaves as if he were in his first job, striving to learn each new process developed in the head office and exported to the Brazilian plant. He saw this as a mechanism for staying in the job, which may explain why he has been with the Brazilian company longer – about nine years – than other Chinese managers. Moreover, the act of making *Guanxi*, which he carries with him since China, making good contacts from different social relationships is highly valued by him. In his perception, ascension in the job market and the possibilities of mobility in the city of Manaus are related mainly to the ability a person has to establish bonds and create networks of friends who work in several different areas in the labor market:

> It is very important to have a friendship network, because this helps a lot. I have friends who are doctors, entrepreneurs, and working in the public sector. For example: a (Brazilian) friend of mine wants to give me a plot of land measuring 10,000 square meters here in rural Amazonas. He wants to give it to me for free. However, I want to see it first. It is in the town of Manacapuru. (And, what does he want in return? Nothing?) Yes, nothing. We will

> invest together. We will plant something. I have no idea yet, but I will see the land first. He is my partner, a businessman friend. I know him very well. He said he will transfer the land to me at the notary office, but I think we will need to make a high investment.
>
> *(Interview with the author, 2016)*

For Nang, trying to create bonds with the place where he lives was important because he aimed to do business in Brazil. He intended to grow some agricultural crops, or even entering the retail trade by opening stores in downtown Manaus that sell Chinese products:

> I want to be an entrepreneur here, because my business is to bring things from China. Therefore, I'm still checking to see what kind of investment I'm going to make. I graduated as an agronomist, but I don't work in this field. Besides, working in a company is very stressful, there is too much pressure to complete a project.
>
> *(Interview with the author, 2016)*

A major impediment to Nang's attempt to establish bonds in the city was the control exerted by the head office over his life. According to Nang, the Chinese at the head office demands a lot from him and does not give him time to relax, even on weekends. When my assistant and I arranged to go out with him on a Saturday afternoon, for example, he said that he could not, and explained: "I have to be in the factory on Saturday to write reports and show them the results we have achieved. I also have to stay there to check on defective machines". On another Saturday, he could only be with us in the evening. This demand made him think, sometimes, about not wanting to work in Brazil anymore: "It is very stressful, a lot of work. We not have much time to do other things here", he said.

In addition, Nang pointed out that his permanence in Brazil would depend on his financial situation and that of his family, because in 2016, for example, his wife and children came to live in Brazil with him[8]:

> I am nearing the top of the hierarchy [company positions]. I don't know if I want another position. I have to figure out what I am going to do, because I still don't have that much money, because now my son is here. He is 7 years old, and every month I have to pay $400.00 for school. I had no other choice. Because he [son] doesn't speak Portuguese, so there [at school] he will learn Portuguese and English. My wife brought Mandarin and English math books to give to my son. Now I really don't know how long I will stay in Manaus. The Brazilian economy is not very good this year. It depends on the financial situation, how it is going to turn out. However, according to locals, if you eat jaraqui,[9] you never leave here, right?
>
> *(Interview with the author, 2016)*

Besides such personal aspects of his life, in many occasions, Nang also addressed labor issues in Brazil, which, according to him, "are very different from China", indicating a duality on how he expressed the capital/labor relationship, either as an expatriate worker or as a manager:

> The Brazilian labor law is very complicated. It is different in China. I think that this is going to hinder Brazil a lot. If it doesn't change, Brazil will be unable to grow. It might sink. But, if the president changes this, he won't win any votes, right? There are workers in the company who become Union representatives just to avoid being fired, because the law gives them stability. We cannot do anything. Some of them sue the company alleging that they are in different jobs than the ones they were hired for. They do it just to make some money. It is not much. I think that if they had been working on something else during the process, which takes a long time, they would make more money. There are many lawsuits here. When I went . . . I went to a trial as a witness, there were a lot of people there. I think it's just to make some money. In China they also have labor laws, but not similar to here. There is no problem with overtime. Overtime is allowed, but here there are many things that the workers complain about. It needs to change to avoid sinking your country.
>
> *(Interview with the author, 2016)*

However, in his view, Brazilian labor laws are good for workers, including him, because the legislation protects the worker: "I like working in Brazil and I think that staying here is probably the best option because I have more rights. However, many rights are bad for Brazil's growth".

As far as the future of the company in Manaus is concerned, besides labor rights that paradoxically were seen by the interviewee as something positive, because they benefit him, at the same time, as something negative, because they hurt the company's profit. Nang showed some concern about the financial and political crisis experienced by the country in 2016 for threatening the way TVChina operationalized its production by routinely importing inputs brought in from China:

> Even though the economy is not doing very well, we continue to make promotions of our products, thereby keeping the volume of production so that our brand becomes more famous every day, even if we lose money in the process. Now, the dollar rate situation is a bad factor for the company because we spend more money to buy dollars. R$5.00 buys only U$S 1.00. We lose a lot with this. This is a bad for the company because we import some products (Emphasis mine). It is only good for those who export, but TVChina only sells its products for the Brazilian domestic market.
>
> *(Interview with the author, 2016)*

Marcos Lee's journey

My third interviewee was Marcos Lee. I met him in 2015 during one of my interviews with Roger Nang, the day he visited the place where I was staying in Manaus, a friend's house. As I mentioned, Nang brought his boss, TVChina's director, Marcos Lee, and I prepared some grilled fish for our lunch. That day, I hardly asked any questions related to my research to avoid exposing Nang to his superior, even though everyone knew that I was studying the Chinese factories in Manaus. The objective there was merely to establish and deepen contacts, so we talked more about me than about them.

Several days after this meeting, I asked Nang to give me Marcos Lee's contact information who, during our lunch, had demonstrated a great deal of knowledge about Brazil and the course of the Chinese economy. A few weeks later, I sent him a message via a cell phone application asking if we could talk about his work in the city of Manaus. Marcos Lee answered yes, but that he would like to do it in person.

At the time, I had returned to São Paulo to attend the remaining courses of my PhD, so I asked if we could have an interview in early 2016, when I would be in Manaus again for field research. With Lee's approval – just making it clear that it would be "a conversation, not an interview" – he set up the meeting place at the same public house where I interviewed Nang in a city shopping mall, and there we talked about various aspects of his life, just the two of us.

The interview did not take long because he had to leave to attend a meeting with his Chinese superiors. Nevertheless, a few days later we talked again, alone, in the same place, this time with more time and more details about his journey as a Chinese worker and expatriate. Similar to the other expatriates, I also kept in touch with Lee through messaging applications, especially when there were questions about some aspect of his life or about company data, to which he always answered me very kindly. Another significant point of the dialogues with Lee was that he informed and confirmed various data regarding expatriate salaries as well as information regarding the Chinese rural/urban environment.

When the first interview took place, Marcos Lee was 35 years old, had been living in Manaus for three years and was the materials/supplies manager, the position responsible for controlling all the products imported to PIM's TVChina. Lee was married and had two children who lived in southern China, in the province of Fujian, a city with a population of 500,000 near Taiwan. Because the company did not provide benefits such as housing to the expatriate who brought his/her family, his wife and children stayed in China and provided support to his parents who lived with them in an apartment in the urban center of the province.

The fact that his parents lived in the urban area and owned a small business – a convenience store – was a source of joy for Lee, something he celebrated as a great victory over the many hardships he and his family had endured in the years when farming was their only source of income.

From those days, Lee remembers that his parents' small farm was like many others owned by poor Chinese peasants, who were granted land plots by the state so that they could develop family-based agriculture. Until 1980, the land did not belong to the individual and his family, but to the village community. Only after this period did a reformulation of the rules occur in China that authorized the individual concession, but only for a period of 70 years, as the land continues to be the property of the State.

In this context in which the family had little land for agriculture, Lee's parents gave priority to the development of a subsistence agriculture selling the surplus, which allowed for his upbringing in the poverty of Chinese countryside.

Under this aspect, Lee reports that his parents, from an early age, taught him to work on the land as a farmer, because that was the fate of young peasants in China. However, despite working in the fields with his parents, they always wanted their son to leave that hard life and, therefore, they saved for his studies the little financial resource left from the farm sales, to give him an opportunity to live away from the rural area:

> My parents were peasants and raised me in the countryside. We grew whatever we could sell, like rice and vegetables, and I helped my parents with the farm work when I was younger. Then, during my school years, I went to the city to study. I had a good education, in a good public high school in the city. Then I went to a public university in a town even further away. I had to leave the countryside for the city because my family was not rich and my father was a peasant. Chinese people *were not* rich many years ago, so parents placed their only hope on their children's good education. That's because if you had a good education you had a chance to go to a good elementary school, to a good high school, and had a better chance of getting into university. Therefore, the parents worked hard as farmers to give their children a chance to improve their lives. When I went to study in the city, I stopped helping them with the farming and they helped me with my studies. Because I had a good opportunity to study, I got job opportunities as well. I had no choice. I had to study!
>
> *(Interview with the author, 2016)*

In China, for a long time, the rural area was associated with limited access to cultural and social goods. That is why Lee's parents strove to give him an opportunity for education in the country's good public schools so that he could have a better future. In 1990, China reformed the migration laws, which encouraged mass displacement of peasants to the coastal cities. It also encouraged his parents to have their son study in the city, permitting Lee, at the age of 24, to graduate with a degree in furniture/interior design from a public university, and get his first job outside the rural areas in a factory manufacturing office furniture.

Even though he was happy to be working, this activity was not exactly what he was looking for. Discouraged by this first job, and after a period of two months without being able to adapt to the type of work he was doing, he learned through his girlfriend – who worked at TVChina – that a large international Chinese company had a position available for people who were fluent in English. Despite the fact that his English level was not excellent, according to him, it was above the average of the other candidates, and that helped him get the new job.

At TVChina's Chinese headquarters, Lee's job did not require much of a college education and he described it as "a lower level, customer service job". However, he saw that through hard work he could grow and change industries over time. Therefore, being a recent graduate with no experience, he tried to work hard in this role in order to stand out and get a better position in the company.

After two years in an area that was not highly valued, an opportunity opened up for Lee to work in a branch located in Poland. As Lee recounted, this was a chance to turn his career around:

> I only had two years of work experience in the company, and I was very new to this area, but it was a very good chance because I was new, I had recently graduated from university, and it would be a good experience, and the salary was better than what I was getting in China. Besides, it was indeed a good chance, because for the past three years promotions were not so easy to happen for the Chinese. So I decided to go because I needed this experience and because I was not a rich man and I needed money to build a future. My parents understood my decision because it was a great chance and my girlfriend (whom I later married) understood. In China it is common culture for men to go in search of money and leave home to get things and be able to help the family, especially in the South of China, everyone does this. Women also understand, because that' s how it is in China, so they consider it normal for the husband to leave home to work in distant places.
>
> *(Interview with the author, 2016)*

Lee accepted the offer and spent four years working in Poland in production planning and sales support positions. At the end of this period, he decided to return to China because he missed his family, but his stay did not last long because the company offered him a new job, as a manager, this time in Brazil. In 2013, Lee moved to the city of Manaus to manage the entire process of product imports from the Chinese headquarters to the Brazilian subsidiary.

Lee and his Chinese colleagues have in mind that going to another country serves primarily to fulfill a mission, much more than being a manager. This was evident in the company's own hierarchy, when Lee and the other interviewees stated that they were subordinated to China – "my boss is China" – and not the local company itself. It is a matrix relationship, as I highlighted earlier. "The supply boss is local, but my general manager is Chinese. However, it is the Brazilian company that pays my salary". And he adds,

> In Brazil, I earn in Real, more than if I were in China, because the salary is lower there. In Brazil, the major benefit I have is the salary, and the second is the experience that I gain, a great gain for my future. Furthermore, I have

> a higher position, and this is very important, because by the time I get back to China I will add to my four years of experience in Poland and another four years in Brazil. In the future, I might have good job opportunities in Chinese companies due to my experience. Another benefit that I have is that my vacation, of 45 days,[10] and fully paid by the company, including my plane ticket to visit my family in China. The company also pays for the apartment where I live here in Manaus.
>
> *(Interview with the author, 2016)*

If, on the one hand, Lee saw this access to benefits and wages obtained in Brazil in a positive way, on the other hand, by 2016, he was already considering returning to China, something that occurred in 2019, when his contract ended and he joined the head office staff, as a production manager:

> It is good for me here in Brazil, we have some benefits. Nevertheless, there is also a lot of work and a lot of pressure from the bosses. There is also the distance. We spend an entire year away from our parents, wife and children. So, when I go to China on vacation, I stay with them all the time, I don't want to get involved with anything from work. I have had a lot of work recently and that is quite tiring.
>
> *(Interview with the author, 2016)*

Between control and autonomy: the limits of disciplined expatriation

The Chinese expatriates interviewed have sought to establish local contacts so they can have, among other things, possible work alternatives at the factory. They realize that their job tenure is also flexible and that it may change at any time, depending on the economic/political situation of the countries where they are, or changes imposed by the head office.

Therefore, when they arrive in Manaus, they try to build networks, first with other Chinese, then with Brazilians, creating bridges that can be useful in the future, as well as in the present. They do *Guanxi*. The strategy seems to be a means of not being so dependent on factory work, but to escape, at some point, the duality between opportunity and sacrifice associated with being a Chinese expatriate.

Opportunity and sacrifice mean that he or she is not just an agent of the factory control. They are also the object of this control, a duality that haunts them throughout the expatriation process, whether in the factory or in the apartments, a place that can be considered, even legally, an enclave of it.

One of the expatriates, an engineer at the TVChina Company, told me that he felt a lot of pressure from headquarters to find ways to implement automation projects in manufacturing to reduce costs and reduce the number of workers. Therefore, outside working hours, he had to stay in the apartment studying technical notions and answering questionnaires sent to him by the company in

China. Another one spoke to me of his fear that the company would discover that he was working on personal projects when he got to the apartment, "because the company demands full dedication from me. But at night I'm running a company with my friend".

This is how the Chinese head office establishes a form to surround the expatriate, to impose limits, and to seek to control his mobility and his life. Nevertheless, the Chinese attempt to create their own expatriation routes and trajectories makes the expatriate's journey in Manaus seem like a mix between control and autonomy.

As elements of control, there are a) the expatriation terms; b) the contract time; c) the expatriate rotation; d) the reporting requirements; e) the housing system in the PIM; and f) the mobility control between China and Manaus.

As characteristics of autonomy, the following are worth pointing out: a) The use of the housing system and mobility control as a way to create solidarity among the expatriates. For example, it occurs through mutual support to the entrepreneurial businesses that they establish in Manaus, as well as in "helping" the family of an expatriate who did not travel to China, but is assisted by another expatriate, who takes them resources and packages. b) Use of the housing system and the services available in the apartments for dedication to one's own economic activities. c) Financial planning, using savings and other financial investments. According to one expatriate, the purpose of this is to save "until I can walk alone". d) Use of the status conferred by expatriation, allowing one to make new contacts important for business in Brazil and for a future business in China. e) Opening of businesses such as stores in downtown Manaus, or "Amazonian goods" sold in China, or even the acquisition of Chinese goods to be sold in Manaus. In this expatriate market, "legal" and "illegal" meet and mix.

By considering these issues, one can move further into Smith & Zheng's (2016) proposition that expatriates are in other productive territories because they are more work-focused and do things that locals do not. There is this aspect. However, one realizes that an "expatriation from below" also occurs, or rather, a tangle of struggles that encompasses the goals of the Chinese parent company and the expatriates' journey on a new path.

Furthermore, learning about who these expatriates are allows us to visualize the dualities that surround this type of labor mobility, corroborating what Knowles (2014) points out, when he says that globalization is fragile and creates uncertainties in life and in the scenarios that it sustains and destabilizes at the same time. It sustains economic logics and destabilizes people. Expatriates are caught in the middle, between sustaining and destabilizing.

Besides the opportunity to go to Manaus, there are also concerns about the social situation in China, those of the parents, wife, and children who stayed on the other side of the globe, due to the restrictions imposed by the type of expatriation set by the companies. There is also the concern about the children's education including how to get the necessary resources for this. In addition, there is homesickness. Despite this, the expatriates seek to overcome the distance and the pressure from the head office, because they want to open new trails, to trace different paths from those that their parents took, during the Mao Zedong era, and their own, in the "new China".

Summary

On the basis of these observations, one can see that *disciplined expatriation* brings to the Amazon a specific type of expatriation, very peculiar in relation to the Western model.

Among these specificities, there is cost reduction with parts of the labor force – managers and coordinators – that in Brazil have salaries much higher than that of the average worker on the factory floor. Besides, these workers are better controlled, given the globalization of the factory dormitory policy, meaning that the expatriates literally have to live for their jobs. There is also the economic impossibility for the Chinese to take their family with them on this trip, because they would lose the benefit of the apartment paid for by the company and the annual trip to China. There is also the element of control that allows the head office to manage the global processes in person, with costs lower than those of other international companies. Finally, there are the consequences of expatriation on the lives of the Chinese, who are placed under the route of capital, but who have a personal trajectory and desires that are not associated with profit, but with hope, fears, desire for social change, and greater autonomy.

Notes

1 Originating in Amazon, the acai bowl is made of frozen acai palm fruit that is pureed and served as a smoothie in a bowl or glass.
2 In the comparisons highlighted here, the Brazilian exchange rate was 2.35.
3 In Smith's sense of the term (2003): dormitory *labour regime*.
4 The names are fictitious, but they follow the structure adopted by the Chinese in Manaus: they use a local or Americanized name as a first name. The second name is the Chinese surname.
5 According to Shang, in 2014, this competition amounted to more than 500 people per opening.
6 According to Shang, women in China are "trained from childhood to endure staying away from their future husbands", so "she (his wife) doesn't get so sad when she is far away from me for a long time".
7 Nang said that when he goes on his vacations to China, he takes with him natural products from the Amazon so that his father can sell them in Chinese trade.
8 In contact with Nang in 2017, he informed me that his wife and son stayed only three months in Brazil. They did not adapt to the climate of the city and the high cost of bilingual school in Manaus.
9 Fish endemic to the Amazon region, highly prized by the local population.
10 Just like Nang, he told us that whenever he goes to China on vacation, he takes propolis extract to his relatives, because in China this type of natural substance is highly prized.

6

CONCLUSION

Toward a global Chinese production model

In today's scenario involving a race to form "little Chinas" around the world, no region of the planet has escaped the clutches of the Asian dragon, not even the Amazon. A space of capitalist economic globalization since the nineteenth century, the region is now a new frontier for the expansion of Chinese business in the southern hemisphere. Therefore, it was against this scenario that I sought to investigate the labor implications of the Chinese factories installed in the Manaus Free Trade Zone.

In the context of labor transformations in Brazil, and the world, the data presented here indicate that the Chinese factories, in terms of labor management, distance themselves from the main managerial practices implemented in the 1990s, and the beginning of the millennium, known as productive restructuring, while simultaneously updating many of its elements. On the other hand, they introduce original issues that, together, constitute what I call the *Chinese production model*. This becomes clearer when summarizing the elements covered throughout the chapters of this volume.

Expatriation is a management cost reduction and global control mechanism for Chinese factories. Although expatriation is a common practice in corporate management, the Chinese method has its own originality and specific reason for its existence.

Among these reasons, the first one is the number of expatriates. In most of the international factories located in Manaus, especially the European and North American ones, the participation of foreign managers is minimal. In these companies, the only reason foreigners come to the city is to provide training, analyze the economic situation, or participate in meetings with ZFM managers. Moreover, even among the oriental companies, such as Japanese, the percentage of expatriates in the total labor force does not exceed 1%, as I highlighted in Chapter 5.

In the factories surveyed, this number exceeds 5%. In wholly state-owned plants, expatriates represent about 10% of the total workforce. A similar situation was seen

DOI: 10.4324/9781003229377-6

by Lee (2009), in Africa, and by Cooke (2012), in India. The latter revealed that expatriates accounted for 30% of the labor force in Chinese factories.

The second reason is the type of worker that is expatriated: managers, coordinators, up to supervisors, revealing the specificity of this expatriation mode, especially when it comes to top positions, something new in the ZFM, that is, expatriation of supervisors as a factory policy.

Given these elements, Chinese expatriation is very specific not only for the amounts of expatriates or the positions they hold in factories but also for its symbolic aspect. In Africa, for example, Lee (2017) notes that Chinese state-owned enterprises have emphasized to expatriates the necessity of "Eating Bitterness", enduring adversity to make China great internationally: "the strength of the expatriate is the strength of China", claim Chinese government representatives.

A similar process was also observed in the Amazon, emphasizing the nationalistic character, always present in the words of the Chinese managers interviewed especially in relation to China's need to overcome poverty and face its regional competitors, such as South Korea and Japan, the latter always remembered by expatriates for having "invaded China" in the past. During this process, overcoming the adversities of expatriation, frugality, sense of duty, and nationalism become highly valued points.

Furthermore, there are differences in relation to the recruitment process of these expatriates, the bureaucratic requirements, the amount of work the expatriates do inside and outside the factories, the salary level lower than that of their Brazilian peers, the policy of "factory dormitories", and the control exercised by the headquarters. I called this whole system *materially and culturally disciplined expatriation.*

Theoretically, this shows that there is a new front of global worker mobility underway with trajectories and interests connecting different world regions. Hence, Chinese expatriation helps to reveal that it is not only capital but labor that becomes more and more global in meaning.

Matrix Taylorism. While in Fordist production management, there was a rigid separation between conception and execution, creating hierarchical spaces between management and operators, in Japanese management, that is, at least discursively, "shared" with the workers who play a "collaborative" role. Under the Chinese model, it structures a factory floor based on "operator production", with operational skill as its central element. This was the point highlighted, mainly in Chapters 3 and 4.

An example of this is that the ability to learn, work motivation, ability to work with colleagues, teamwork, and collaborative work, which characterized the Japanese model, are no longer fundamental in Chinese organizational management. Thinking becomes the management's role. Implementing is the workers' job. In this sense, the Chinese model recovers practices from the Taylorist form of Fordism, but on a new basis: *matrix Taylorism.* For example, separation between management and workers is due to the control exercised by the "headquarters" that matrixly controls their overseas managers. Therefore, they have less freedom to relate with the local shop floor.

In other words, it is not a scientific philosophy of organization, as advocated by Taylorism, but an influence of the political/state control and project on the manufacturing processes, a result of China's own culture and economic/projected system. In addition to these aspects, Chinese managers are expatriate workers, which, from the very beginning, implies greater linguistic and cultural difficulties in their relationship with the employees. This is exemplified by the rigid information control that is not shared with the Brazilians, including those in the same hierarchical position, as we have seen throughout the book.

Furthermore, it is also necessary for these managers to stand out in Brazil in order to be able to occupy higher positions and face the strong competition in factories located in China, leading to an unbridled race for production results, ignoring managerial issues. Furthermore, their short permanence in Brazil and the biannual rotation of expatriate managers mean that bonds between managers and workers are not created, or at least solidified. Something that is further aggravated because the newly arrived expatriates arriving in Manaus bring a factory floor mentality from China, more technical and less "participative".

In addition, it is important to note that expatriates are not trained to be "managers" as in the West. As discussed in Chapter 5, in general, these managers are technicians who excel in China and after a long selection process are approved to move to factories in other countries. Proud of their new status, they start to manage with a focus on "technical worker"and the ability of the workforce to seek his own qualification, and not on the education and training of leaders or management policies of incentives.

Another element that corroborates this separation between managers and workers is the *controlled dormitory policy*. As emphasized, the Chinese expatriates do not have their own housing in the places where they are sent to. They share apartments with up to five other Chinese co-workers, something cultural from China's factory floor and, given its context, reproduced in many Chinese globalized factories.

As observed by Smith & Zheng (2016) and Lee (2017) concerning Chinese FDI in Europe and Africa, expatriates do not have much time to relate to each other, to integrate with local society, or even to share moments of fraternization with the workers inside or outside the factory. In general, they live to perform work related to the technical aspect of the job, without much contact with management training.

Finally, there is a hierarchical dimension inherent to social relations among the Chinese based on Guanxi, a cultural practice that permeates the most diverse forms of social interaction in China (Pinheiro-Machado 2011), and on *nationalism as a project*, something embraced by expatriates. This is part of the Chinese model and is expressed by the strict separation between Chinese managers and local workers, the symbolic prevailing over the monetary, the negotiations watered by personal need for trust, the exchange of favors, frugality, and the sense of duty of Chinese individual in Manaus.

Global factories with production regionalization, but without deterritorialization. Unlike flexible capitalism's global capital, Chinese capital expands throughout the world, without deterritorializing production. Among the reasons explaining this "Chinese characteristic", I highlight the fact that at least for the time being, there is no international division of labor promoted by China, as occurred with global production in the 1970s onward (center and periphery of production).

Back then, multinational corporations moved to other countries, leaving the design or most technological aspects of the production processes in their country of origin. However, when dealing with the current moment, of Chinese globalization, in general, China is moving abroad, but implementing in its subsidiaries the same things that happen in its own territory, as highlighted in Chapters 3 and 4. This shows that, as seen during the interviews, what happens in Manaus is a process previously tested and operationalized on the Chinese headquarters' factory floor. Indeed, machines and equipment in the production process are routinely transferred to the Manaus factories under the supervision of "missions" from Chinese technicians. Indeed, machines and equipment used in the production process are routinely transferred to the factories in Manaus under the supervision of Chinese technicians on "missions".

Therefore, Chinese expansion is a global project, but strongly rooted in China. This explains why low- and high-tech production processes coexist in the country with robotic production lines, as well as with those that require a high demand for manual labor. Therefore, it is clear that Chinese factories abroad continue to be, in many ways, a "copy" of what happens in China itself.

Non-deterritorialization manifests itself not only in production but also in management. I mean this in reference to the fact that, even though the Chinese managers are in Manaus, they do not lose their productive territoriality with China. This is a "shared" management, of control and organization as if it were a single productive territory. The manager has a double function: organize the factory in Manaus and work tirelessly for the head office by sending reports, both electronically and in person, elements discussed in Chapter 5.

The return to direct supervision over workers. According to Taylor's principle of production organization, the worker intentionally tended to idleness and slowness, hence the necessity for management to provide functional work supervision to increase company productivity. Under the Japanese model, the idea of worker "autonomy" and "indirect supervision" was emphasized, and control was exercised in a subjective way.

The Chinese model returns to direct supervision, but with new contours and contexts. Among these, what attracts attention is the fact that supervision is exercised from China all the way down to the local factory floor. Therefore, it is not a question of a strict worker supervision, but of the factory itself, and this is at a global level. So, there is direct supervision in production, but it results from the global supervision exercised by the Chinese headquarters. In practical terms, as we saw throughout the book, the head office supervises the manager, who supervises the technicians and the operators.

Furthermore, we are not facing a supervision based on "moral coercion", something inherent to the scientific managerial style advocated by Taylor – basis of Western production rationalization – but of a political/bureaucratic control embedded in China's economic and social formation, which also affects its factories. A supervision that originates from the top, from the country's political/social format, as a political science, and not as an administration science.

Another element that helps to clarify this process used in the Chinese factories is the "transfer of assembly lines" from China to Manaus. When they are transferred to the ZFM, supervisors are relocated to inspect whether the process is being well adapted or not. The reverse also occurs, although to a lesser extent. Production lines with good productivity in Manaus can serve as a model for production lines located in China; therefore, supervisors are essential to provide feedback to Chinese managers, something that I emphasized in Chapter 4. Production processes that "work" in China should work in Manaus as well. Thus, the role of the supervisors consists in making Manaus and China a single productive and manageable territory.

The export/import policy of inputs. In theory, the inputs necessary for Chinese production would be a dependency or a vulnerability that generates some negotiation or bargaining in PIM. However, unlike other FDI, the Chinese model works to create a dependency that it meets through Chinese exporting companies.

In Manaus, the local political bargain for Chinese investments (or other investments) is almost nil, because the ZFM's economic model depends on FDI, without many counterparts, especially when it comes to the Chinese productive leverage. A good example is how strongly imports from this country have been growing in the ZFM, going from a little more than 10% in 1997 to almost 50% in 2015. In the companies surveyed, about 90% of the imported inputs have a foreign origin. Furthermore, the imported inputs (use values) are also transformed locally into exchange values, as I pointed out in Chapter 3. Thus, the Chinese model is also characterized by the *global coordination of production and export of inputs.*

Matrix factories that are nationally engaged and heavy. Due to the dependence on political/state control exercised by China, the number of Chinese players interested in FDI and the weight it represents in the implementation of investments in other territories, the mobility of capital, changes in production processes and responses to changing circumstances are not as "flexible" as seen in other global Western investments. This is mainly explained by the bureaucratic chain that goes from the factory floor to the head office, as well as by the political/economic control and governmental strategy related to these Chinese investments.

With systems that have some autonomy but that respond to a central command, each Chinese FDI is fitted within a system of planning, control, and economic/political management that makes Chinese factories "heavier" than factories of Western flexible capitalism. The regionalization of Chinese factories in certain territories is more complex than the process of "productive decentralization" that occurred in the West at the end of the twentieth century. This lack of flexibility can be beneficial or disastrous for those places that receive Chinese investments, which depends, on the one hand, on China's interests in the region and, on the other, on the local ability to negotiate with Chinese capital.

According to Lee (2017), the installation of Chinese factories in Africa relates to relations that started in the 1960s, involving political and geostrategic needs, beyond economics. As a result, the flight of capital, due to the 2008 crisis, was less intense for Chinese capital, because the cost of mobility would be higher than that of staying in the region. This is also why Chinese companies in Zambia and Tanzania, despite losses or very low profit margins, continued to operate, given the "political profit" of Chinese expansion in the African territory.

In relation to Manaus, the Chinese FDI "inflexibility" has resulted in little local rooting. With no "political and geostrategic needs" in its relationship with ZFM, and due to the latter's incapacity to bargain with the Asian country, the weight of Chinese "inflexibility" becomes, in this case, an obstacle to advances in the organization of work in the factories in the PIM. With the pendulum swinging more toward control rigidity and matrix interests, these companies have found it very difficult to make changes, to adapt to the local context of laws, and to make working in the ZFM less "technical" and bureaucratic. An example of this is the little leeway that Brazilian managers have in local decision-making, especially in matters that involve HR, which responds directly to China-based "headquarters".

As a result, it is evident that the Chinese factories are more strongly linked to China than to Manaus, which creates difficulties in relationships with local labor unions, workers, and suppliers. The result is a set of factory sites that are poorly rooted, less flexible, without much negotiation, and almost independent from supplies in the city, with no political agenda in investments, and no needs to create local bonds.

Consequently, it is one more *Made in China* and one less *Produced in Manaus*, with little gain for labor.

Certainly, this study has its limits, and its primary objective is to reveal the type of work promoted by Chinese factories on Brazilian soil; but the empirical data outlined here, associated with the theoretical syntheses outlined, point out that the issue of Global China also implies a production model with basic characteristics found all over the planet. And this occurs both by the necessity of reproduction of the Chinese industrial system, matrixly and politically coordinated, and by the counterposition of this system to Western managerial practices dominant in the twentieth century, which gained relative autonomy in relation to politics and the national issue.

In summary, there is no Global China without a global Chinese production model to support it as an industrial practice. Hence, the need for further empirical studies to map the unfolding, in several contexts, of Chinese managerial and industrial practices, to reveal more elements and characteristics of a Chinese model of production with global dimensions.

It is also necessary to expand the study in Brazil, to map the different types of capital in Chinese factories that may present different indicators of salaries, benefits, absenteeism, turnover, and labor disputes. And also, how Maoism, Leninism, Marxism, Confucianism, Taoism, and the Guanxi system influence, in a broad sense, the Chinese management style. Finally, the trajectory of expatriates in

Manaus and their insertion in the city is something to be developed. Likewise, it would be important to observe which are the new paths developed by those expatriates who returned to China.

These are topics for more research to expand the understanding of this new historical momentum: that of Chinese globalization.

WORKS CITED

AGUIAR, Diana. (2017), *A Geopolítica de Infraestrutura da China na América do Sul: um estudo a partir do caso do Tapajós na Amazônia brasileira* (1st ed.). Rio de Janeiro: ActionAid Brasil/ FASE.

ANDRADE, Allison. (2014), *Como se produzem "colaboradores"? Entre prática de gestão e intensificação do trabalho no polo duas rodas em Manaus*. Master's thesis in sociology, Universidade Federal do Amazonas, Manaus.

ANDRIJASEVIC, Rutvica, & SACCHETTO, Devi. (2016), Foxconn beyond China: Capital-labour relations as co-determinants of internationalization. In: *China at Work: A Labour Perspective on the Transformation of Work and Employment in China*. Liu, M., & Smith, C. (eds.). London: Palgrave.

APPADURAI, Arjun. (1996), *Modernity at Large: Cultural Dimensions of Globalization*. Minneapolis, MN: University of Minnesota Press.

ARRIGHI, Giovanni. (2007), *Adam Smith in Beijing: Lineages of the Twenty-First Century*. London: Verso.

BIATO JUNIOR, Oswaldo. (2010), *A parceria estratégica Sino-Brasileira: origens, evolução e perspectivas (1993–2006)*. Brasília: FUNAG.

BODOMO, A. (2019), Is China colonizing Africa? Africa – China relations in a shifting Global Economic Governance system. In: *Global Economic Governance and Human Development*. Raudino, S., & Poletti, A. (eds.). Abingdon: Routledge. 120–132.

BOURDIEU, Pierre. (1977), *Outline of a Theory of Practice*. Cambridge: Cambridge University Press.

BOURDIEU, Pierre. (1996), *The Rules of Art, Genesis and Structure of the Literary Field*. Cornwall: Stanford University Press.

BURAWOY, M. (1979), *Manufacturing Consent*. Chicago, IL: University of Chicago Press.

BURGOON, B., & RAESS, D. (2014), Chinese investment and European labor: Should and do workers fear Chinese FDI? *Asia Europe Journal*, 12 (1–2), 179–197.

BURLAMAQUI, Leonardo. (2015), As finanças globais e o desenvolvimento financeiro chinês: um modelo de governança financeira global conduzido pelo estado. In: *China em transformação: dimensões econômicas e geopolíticas do desenvolvimento* (1st ed.). Cintra, M.A., Silva Filho, E.B., & Costa Pinto, E. (Org.). Brasília: IPEA.

ČANĚK, Marek. (2016), Building the European Centre in Czechia: Foxconn's local integration in regional and global labour market. In: *Flexible Workforces and Low Profit Margins: Electronics Assembly between Europe and China*. ANDRIJASEVIC, Rutvica, & SACCHETTO, Devi (eds.). Brussels: European Trade Union Institute (ETUI).

CARDOSO DE OLIVEIRA, Roberto. (2000), *O trabalho do antropólogo* (2nd ed.). São Paulo, SP: Ed. Unesp.

CARIELLO, Tulio. (2021), Investimentos chineses no Brasil: histórico, tendências e desafios globais (2007–2020). *Conselho Empresarial Brasil-China*. www.institutoconfucio.com.br/wp-content/uploads/2021/08/INVESTIMENTOS_CHINA_BRASIL_2007-2020_.pdf (Accessed March 8, 2022).

CHAN, Jenny, & PUN, Ngai. (2010), Suicide as protest for the new generation of Chinese migrant workers: Foxconn, global capital and the State. *The Asia-Pacific Journal: Japan Focus*, 37 (2), https://apjjf.org/-Jenny-Chan/3408/article.html (Accessed January 30, 2017).

CHANGHONG, Pei. (2004), Revisão e Panorama da Reestruturação Econômica da China. In: *Abrindo os olhos para a China*. Belucce Bellucci (Org.). Rio de Janeiro: Educam.

CHEN, Chao-Chuan, & LEE, Yueh-Ting. (2008), Introduction: The diversity and dynamism of Chinese philosophies on leadership. In: *Leadership and Management in China: Philosophies, Theories, and Practices*. Chen, Chao-Chuan, & Lee, Yueh-Ting (eds.). Cambridge: Cambridge University Press.

CHEN, Min. (2004), *Asian Management Systems: Chinese, Japanese and Korean Styles of Business*. London: Thomson Learning.

CHINA LABOUR BULLETIN. (2010), Swimming against the tide. A short history of labour conflict in China and the Government's attempts to control it. *Research Notes*, October 2010. https://clb.org.hk/sites/default/files/archive/en/File/research_reports/Labour%20Conflict%20Report%20final.pdf

CINTRA, M.A., & PINTO, E.C. (2017), China em transformação: transição e estratégias de desenvolvimento. *Review of Political Economy*, 37 (2), 381–400.

COOKE, F.L. (2012), *Human Resource Management in China: New Trends and Practices*. London: Routledge.

CUNHA, André Moreira, & ACIOLY, Luciana. (2009), China: Ascensão à condição de potência global – Características e implicações. In: *Trajetórias recentes de desenvolvimento: estudos de experiências internacionais selecionadas*. CARDOSO, J.R., & José Celso, et al. (org.). Brasília: IPEA.

ESCHER, Fabiano, & WILKINSON, John. (2019), A economia política do complexo Soja-Carne Brasil-China. *Revista de Economia e Sociologia Rural*, 57 (4), 656–678.

GAETANO, Arianne M. (2015), *Out to Work: Migration, Gender, and TBE Changing Lives of Rural Women in Contemporary China*. Honolulu, HI: University of Hawaii Press.

GALLAGHER, M. (2005), *Contagious Capitalism: Globalization and the Politics of Labor in China*. Princeton, NJ and Oxford: Princeton University Press.

GAO, Y. (2004), *Chinese Migrants and Forced Labour in Europe*. Geneva: International Labour Organisation.

GEERTZ, Clifford. (1973), *The Interpretation of Cultures*. New York: Basic Books.

GONDIM, L., & LIMA, J.C. (2006), *A pesquisa como artesanato intelectual: considerações sobre método e bom senso*. São Carlos: EdUFSCar.

GRANOVETTER, Mark S. (1973), The strength of weak ties. *The American Journal of Sociology*, 78 (6), 1360–1380.

GUOYNG, Dang. (2004), Realizações agrícolas e reformas rural na Nova China. In: *Abrindo os olhos para a China*. Belucce Bellucci (Org.). Rio de Janeiro: Educam.

HAIRONG, Yan, & SAUTMAN, Barry. (2012), Chasing ghosts: Rumours and representations of the export of Chinese convict labour to developing countries. *The China Quarterly*, 210 (2), 398–418.

HALL, S. (1992), The question of cultural identity. In: *Modernity and Its Futures*. Hall, S., Held, D., & McGrew, T. (eds.). Milton Keynes, Cambridge: Open University Press.

HUMPHREY, John. (1995), O impacto das técnicas japonesas de administração sobre o trabalho industrial no Brasil. In: *A máquina e o equilibrista: inovações na indústria automobilística brasileira*. CASTRO, Nádia Araújo de (org.). Rio de Janeiro: Paz e Terra.

HUNG, Ho-fung. (2018), A ascensão da China, a Ásia e o sul global. *Revista de Economia Contemporânea*, 22 (1), 1–26.

JABBOUR, Elias. (2012), *China hoje: Projeto nacional, desenvolvimento e socialismo de Mercado* (1st ed.). São Paulo: Anita Garibaldi: Fundação Maurício Grabois; Paraíba: EDUEPB.

JIA, Wenjuan. (2016), The making of a dualistic labour regime: Changing labour process and power relations in a Chinese state-owned enterprise under globalization. In: *China at Work: A Labour Perspective on the Transformation of Work and Employment in China*. LIU, Mingwei, & SMITH, Chris (eds.). London: Palgrave.

JIANZHOU, L. (2006), Research on labour relations in state-owned enterprises under the new model: An analysis of the manager's. *Perspective Academic Exploration*, 4, 19–26.

JOSEPHS, Hilary K. (1995), Labor law in a 'socialist market economy: The case of China. *Columbia Journal of Transnational Law*, 33, 559–581.

KNOWLES, Caroline. (2014), *Flip-flop: A Journey through Globalisation's Backroads*. Londres: Pluto Press.

LEÃO, R. (2011), A articulação produtiva asiática e os efeitos da emergência chinesa. In *A China na nova configuração global: impactos políticos e econômicos*. LEÃO, R.P.F., PINTO, E.C., & ACIOLY, L. (Orgs). Brasília: IPEA.

LEE, Ching Kwan. (1999), From organized dependence to disorganized despotism: Changing labor regimes in Chinese factories. *The China Quarterly*, 157, 44–71.

LEE, Ching Kwan. (2007), *Against the Law: Labor Protests in China's Rustbelt and Sunbelt*. Berkeley, CA: University of California Press.

LEE, Ching Kwan. (2009), Raw encounters: Chinese managers, African workers and the politics of casualization in Africa's Chinese enclaves. *The China Quarterly*, 199, 647–666.

LEE, Ching Kwan. (2017), *The Specter of Global China: Politics, Labor and Foreign Investment in Africa*. Chicago, IL: University of Chicago Press.

LIMA, Jacob Carlos, & CONSERVA, Marinalva de Sousa. (2006), Redes sociais e mercado de trabalho: entre o formal e o informal. *Política e Trabalho – Revista de Ciências Sociais*, 24, 73–98.

LIMA, Jacob Carlos, & VALLE, M.I.M. (2013), Espaços da globalização: Manaus e as fábricas na Amazônia. *Revista Contemporânea*, 3 (1), 73–88.

LIN, Lefeng. (2016), Workers under disorganized despotism: A case from the state-owned shipbuilding Industry. In: *China at Work: A Labour Perspective on the Transformation of Work and Employment in China*. LIU, Mingwei, & SMITH, Chris (eds.). London: Palgrave.

LIU, Mingwei. (2010), Union organizing in China: Still a monolithic labor movement? *Industrial and Labor Relations Review*, 64 (1), 30–52.

LU, Mengjie. (2016), Control and consent in the process of employee participation in a Chinese state-owned enterprise: The case of BZ iron and steel company. In: *China at Work: A Labour Perspective on the Transformation of Work and Employment in China*. LIU, Mingwei, & SMITH, Chris (eds.). London: Palgrave.

LÜTHJE, B., LUO, S., & ZHANG, H. (2013), *Beyond the Iron Rice Bowl: Regimes of Production and Industrial Relations in China*. Chicago, IL: University of Chicago Press.

MACIEL BRITO, Cleiton. (2017), *Made in China/Produzido no Polo Industrial da Zona Franca de Manaus: o trabalho nas fábricas chinesas*. Doctoral thesis in sociology, Universidade Federal de São Carlos, São Carlos.

MASIERO, Gilmar. (2006), Origens das township and village enterprises (TVEs) Chinesas. *Revista de Economia Política*, 26 (103), 425–444.

MEUNIER, S. (2012), *Political Impact of Chinese Foreign Direct Investment in the European Union on Transatlantic Relations*. Brussels: European Parliament.

MOREIRA, Maurício M. (2005), O desafio Chinês e a indústria na América Latina. *Novos Estudos*, 72, 21–32.

MORENO, Camila. (2015), *O Brasil Made in China: para pensar as reconfigurações do capitalismo contemporâneo*. São Paulo: Fundação Rosa Luxemburgo.

NASCIMENTO, Lucas Gualberto do, & MAYNETTO, Mônica Esmeralda. (2019), One belt, one road: A iniciativa chinesa de infraestrutura e a sua repercussão no BRICS. *BJIR*, Marília, 8 (1), 117–141.

NGOK, K. (2008), The changes of Chinese labour policy and labour legislation in the context of market transition. *International Labour and Working-Class History*, 73 (1), 45–64.

OLIVEIRA, G. de L. T. (2018), A resistência à apropriação chinesa de terras no Brasil desde 2008: lições e alternativas agroecológicas. *Ideias*, 9 (2), 99–132. https://periodicos.sbu.unicamp.br/ojs/index.php/ideias/article/view/8655285 (Accessed January 25, 2022).

OLIVEIRA, Selma Suely Baçal de. (2007), *A "periferia" do capital na cadeia produtiva de eletro-eletrônicos*. Manaus: EDUA.

PINHEIRO-MACHADO, Rosana. (2011), Fazendo Guanxi: dádivas, etiquetas e emoções na economia da China Pós-Mao. *Mana*, 17 (1), 99–130.

PINHEIRO-MACHADO, Rosana. (2017), *Counterfeit Itineraries in the Global South: The Human Consequences of Piracy in China and Brazil*. London and New York: Routledge.

PIRES, Marcos Cordeiro. (2009), Os desafios da concorrência chinesa para a economia brasileira. In: *Nós e a China: o impacto da presença chinesa no Brasil e na América do Sul*. PAULINO, L., & PIRES, Marcos Cordeiro (Orgs). São Paulo: LCTE Editora.

POTTER, P.B., & JIANYONG, L. (1996), Regulating labour relations in China: The challenge of adapting to the socialist market economy. *Les Cahiers de droit*, 37 (3), 753–775.

PUN, N. (2005), *Made in China: Women Factory Workers in a Global Workplace*. Durham, NC: Duke University Press.

PUN, N., & CHAN, J. (2012), Global capital, the state, and Chinese workers: The Foxconn experience. *Modern China*, 38 (4), 383–410. http://www.jstor.org/stable/23216953 (Accessed February 20, 2017).

RAMALHO, J.R. (1997), Precarização do trabalho e impasses da organização coletiva no Brasil. In: *Neoliberalismo, trabalho e sindicatos*. ANTUNUES, R. (ed.). São Paulo: Boitempo.

SACCHETTO, Devi, & ANDRIJASEVIC, Rutvica. (2016), The case of Foxconn in Turkey: Benefiting from free labour and anti-union policy. In: *Flexible Workforces and Low Profit Margins: Electronics Assembly between Europe and China*. Brussels: European Trade Union Institute (ETUI).

SALAZAR, João Pinheiro. (1992), *O novo proletariado industrial de Manaus e as transformações sociais possíveis (estudo de um grupo de operários)*. Doctoral thesis in Sociology, Universidade de São Paulo, São Paulo.

SARAIVA, Miriam Gomes, & SILVA, Álvaro Vicente Costa. (2019), Ideologia e pragmatismo na política externa de Jair Bolsonaro. *Relações Internacionais*, 64, 117–13.

SERÁFICO, Marcelo. (2011), *Globalização e empresariado: estudo sobre a Zona Franca de Manaus*. São Paulo: Annablume.

SILVA, Marilene Corrêa. (2013), *Metamorfoses da Amazônia* (2nd ed.). Manaus: Editora Valer.

SMITH, C. (2003), Living at work: Management control and the dormitory labour system in China. *Asia Pacific Journal of Management*, 20 (3), 333–358 (Accessed April 29, 2022).

SMITH, C., & PUN, N. (2006), The dormitory labour regime in China as a site for control and resistance. *The International Journal of Human Resource Management*, 17 (8), 1456–1470. https://doi.org/10.1080/09585190600804762 (Accessed April 18, 2022).

SMITH, Chris, & LIU, Mingwei. (2016), In search of the labour process perspective in China. In: *China at Work: A Labour Perspective on the Transformation of Work and Employment in China*. LIU, Mingwei, & SMITH, Chris (eds.). London: Palgrave.

SMITH, Chris, & ZHENG, Yu. (2016), The management of labour in Chinese MNCs operating outside of China: A critical review. In: *China at Work: A Labour Perspective on the Transformation of Work and Employment in China*. LIU, Mingwei, & SMITH, Chris (eds.). London: Palgrave.

TANG, Charles. (2017), Investimentos chineses no setor energético brasileiro: oportunidades para o Brasil. *Boletim de Conjuntura do Setor Energético*. FVG Energia, 4–6. https://bibliotecadigital.fgv.br/dspace/bitstream/handle/10438/19276/Coluna%20Opiniao%20Agosto%20-%20Charles%20Tang.pdf (Accessed November 12, 2021).

VALLE, Izabel. (2007), *Globalização e reestruturação produtiva: um estudo sobre a produção offshore em Manaus*. Manaus: Editora da Universidade Federal do Amazonas.

VELHO, G. (1981), *Individualismo e cultura: notas para uma antropologia da sociedade contemporânea*. Rio de Janeiro: Zahar.

WU, B., & LIU, H. (2014), Bringing class back in: Class consciousness and solidarity amongst Chinese migrant workers in Italy and the UK. *Ethnic and Racial Studies*, 37 (8), 1391–1408. www.tandfonline.com/doi/pdf/10.1080/01419870.2012.715660 (Accessed April 15, 2022).

ZEMIN, Jiang. (2002), *Reforma e construção da China*. Rio de Janeiro: Record.

ZHANG, Kevin H. (2006), *China as the World Factory*. New York: Routledge.

INDEX